girlfriends
for life

Other books by
Carmen Renee Berry and Tamara Traeder

girlfriends: Invisible Bonds, Enduring Ties
(Wildcat Canyon Press, 1995)

The girlfriends Keepsake Book:
The Story of Our Friendship
(Wildcat Canyon Press, 1996)

girlfriends Talk About Men:
Sharing Secrets for a Great Relationship
(Wildcat Canyon Press, 1997)

girlfriends
for life

Friendships Worth Keeping Forever

CARMEN RENEE BERRY AND TAMARA TRAEDER

WILDCAT CANYON PRESS
A Division of Circulus Publishing Group, Inc.
Berkeley, California

girlfriends for life: Friendships Worth Keeping Forever
Copyright © 1998 by Carmen Renee Berry and Tamara C. Traeder
Cover image © Owen Franken/Corbis
"Women Speak" by Vicky Edmonds reprinted with permission of
Roy M. Carlisle

Publisher: Julienne Bennett
Editor: Roy M. Carlisle
Copyeditor: Karyn S. DiCastri
Cover and Interior Design: Gordon Chun Design
Typesetting: Holly A. Taines
Typographic Specifications: Body text set in Cochin 11.5/14.5. Heads
set in Cochin.

Printed in the United States of America

Library of Congress Cataloging-in-Publication Data
Berry, Carmen Renee.
    Girlfriends for life: friendships worth keeping forever / Carmen
Renee Berry and Tamara Traeder.
    p.   cm.
ISBN 1-885171-32-3 (pbk.: alk. paper)
        1. Female friendship. 2. Female friendship—Case studies. 3.
Women—Psychology. I. Traeder, Tamara, 1960-   . II. Title.
BF575.F66B447   1999
302.3'4'082—dc21   99-12220   CIP

Distributed to the trade by Publishers Group West
10 9 8 7 6 5 4 3 2 1

*To my childhood girlfriends, Alice and Cynthia —
courageous, fiesty, and loving women — in honor of thirty-
five years of friendship, and in anticipation of at least
thirty-five more.*
—Carmen

*To Laura, my loyal, funny, honest girlfriend for life.
You are invaluable.*
—Tamara

Contents

Acknowledgments

A hearty "thank you" goes to all the women who mailed, faxed, and e-mailed their girlfriend stories to us, tales that gave homage to the friends who have demonstrated how powerfully enduring the girlfriend bond can be. Their stories show that in a world of unpredictable change, solace can be found in these solid relationships that withstand the test of time.

Carmen and Tamara give a hug of gratitude to those incredible women who hung in there with us while we (once again) disappeared from view to write about the benefits of friendship—Laura, Linda, Wynn, Lynn, Cathy, Kathy, Gail, Rene, Renee, Pat, Marianne, Connie, Carolyn, Bobette, Irene, Cynthia, and Alice. Knowing that when we emerged from this project you would be there to welcome us back into the joys of "girlfriendhood" gave us the umph we needed.

For believing in us long before we became writers and for bragging on us after, we thank Mary Ellen Berry and Fern and Gus Traeder. Your support and love means everything to us.

The team at Circulus Publishing Group, Inc. has proven once again that it is the best in the business. Thanks to Julienne Bennett for her encouragement and faith in us, and Leyza Yardley for her skill and diligence in keeping track of all the pieces. For weathering the rough seas only an editor can know, we are grateful to Roy M. Carlisle. You've guided another book safely into the harbor.

Introduction

We've laughed, cried, been so angry we don't speak for a while, but through it all she is the constant in my life. I know I can count on her no matter what, and she'll always be there for me. I know she feels the same.

—DEBBIE CALLAS

Wow! That is the only way we can express our amazement at the response of women to our book, *girlfriends*. We knew that the experience of friendship was a vital part of our own development, but we did not know quite how universal the experience was among other women. Dorothy, one woman who wrote us from Indiana, illustrated this point by recalling, "I bought the *girlfriends* book, and I stopped at an interesting little restaurant and started to read while waiting for my food to arrive. The waitress asked me what I was so absorbed in, and I showed her the book. She sat down, and we had a wonderful conversation, telling each other about the friends we have that we love so much. We both had tears in our eyes and enjoyed sharing

1

the feelings, laughs, and precious moments we each have had with our girlfriends. We both felt very enriched after our conversation."

As if finally believing someone would listen, we received a deluge of letters from women telling us their own girlfriend stories. As we read these letters, offering stories of everyday friendship, we were often moved to tears, or laughter. We were awed by what women do for each other, and we felt a rush of joy knowing this kind of bond is shared by so many. Many women expressed their appreciation for how the book *girlfriends* allowed them the opportunity to take time to think about and celebrate these important relationships in their lives; some went on to tell us that they felt it gave them permission to be a woman and to enjoy womanly things. Karen, from Illinois, shared with us, "Before I read the book I always became irritated at women who celebrated being women. I thought tea parties and makeup and slumber parties were stupid. I grew up in a small town where women who celebrated their femininity were teased and denied privileges because of their gender. I hated acting feminine, dressing like a woman, behaving like a woman, just doing anything that was associated with being female. I have always been afraid of being denied privileges because of my gender, so I denied my femininity in an effort to avoid that fate.

"Now that I've read your book, I've learned that being a woman is something that should be celebrated. I want to enjoy tea parties, jewelry, and dresses. Loving and celebrating these things aren't going to hurt me, but denying them will and did for a long time. I want to thank you for helping me come to my senses. I am much more free with myself in relationships and at my job. My life has improved one hundred percent because of your insight and the insights of all the women who told their stories in your book. Thank you!!" Femininity means different things to different women, but being able to celebrate your own womanhood helps you celebrate your women friends.

We were moved by the responses we received from women all around the world, women who told us how the book affected them or how it reflected their own experiences of friendship. The stories we received were as varied as the women themselves: some told about friends they have known since they were babies, others told about friends they met a relatively short time ago. Having a friend worth keeping for life does not require that we know each other from childhood, that we be the same age (although many friends are), that we share similar traits (although many friends do), or even that we like each other at first (although many are immediately drawn to each other).

While some women described themselves as "even

looking like" their friends, others have found common ground despite their differences, describing a sort of "odd couple" relationship with their friends. Aimee, from Vermont, wrote us, "My girlfriend is Taiwanese and five foot two, I am Italian and five foot eleven, but even though we come from vastly different backgrounds, we click." Neither cultural diversity nor vertical challenges could keep these girlfriends from finding each other.

Physical distance does not seem to matter, either. Peggy, from Texas, shared with us that she has not yet met her friend Eddy, though they have been friends for decades, "Eddy and I have never met face-to-face, never been in the presence of the other, even though we've been pen pals for over thirty years. In 1962, her sixth-grade English teacher and my sixth-grade English teacher traded class rolls in an exchange-student project.

"My pen pal turned out to be a slender, blond girl named Edwinna (Eddy). Our early letters included information about favorite subjects in school, hobbies, pets, things that twelve year olds deem important. As we matured, our letters reflected different concerns: from bodily changes, boys, dating, graduation, and college, to marriage, kids, jobs, and empty nests, and loss of parents, estate planning, and arthritis soon to come. Our loyalty has motivated us to continue writing; our love has allowed us to continue writing."

The friendships that intrigued us the most were the ones that endured the many life events and changes that stress our commitment or estrange us over the years. So many obstacles can interfere with a friendship — geographical distance, illness, brilliant success — and yet some relationships not only survive but flourish for a lifetime. With so many different patterns to friendship, how is it that some friendships survive life's changes, tragedies, and complexities? Why do some friendships endure while others give way under pressure? Drawing from letters and interviews, we try to answer the question that we are most frequently asked: *What qualities make friendships last?*

Certain circumstances and characteristics seem to be common among enduring friendships. We narrowed the many facets of long-lasting friendship into four general characteristics: Connection, Caring, Commitment, and Courage. Not every relationship has every aspect of all four, and some may have additional strengths, but we found, by reading letters from and talking with hundreds of women from around the world, that these four aspects are common and universal.

We also discovered that some women are better trained for friendship than others and may be more skilled in maintaining lasting connections with their girlfriends. Those with one or more models of friendship (women in their lives who demonstrated the importance of female connections) have the advantage of having seen friendships in action. So, what may seem instinctive about how we relate to our friends may come more from having mothers, aunts, and other adult women in our lives who have shown us how to be good friends and how to accept friendship. As Sandra, from Pennsylvania, wrote, "Throughout my life, I have been blessed with the most wonderful friends. Some are forever friends, and some were friends of specific stages and seasons. This need for close friendships comes from my mother. By her example, she taught me to make and keep friends. At the age of seventy-eight, she still has friends that she met decades ago."

This insight is echoed in another letter we received, in which Tracey, from Georgia, concluded: "I cannot end this letter without paying tribute to the women who taught me that 'to have a friend is to be a friend', my mother and grandmother. There are not words to express the love and gratitude I feel for being a part of their legacy of friendship. It has created more joy in my life than they will ever know. They taught me how to look at people with my heart and not my eyes. Because of that gift, I have cried many tears of sorrow as well as joy, but I would not trade one of those tears for a life less troubled by the tears of my friends." So the secret is out — women learn from other women — and we learn not only how to live our lives as females but how to be skilled girlfriends.

But whether or not a woman was trained from an early age to be a good friend and to recognize the necessary qualities for friendship in others, it is never too late to learn. If we did not find role models in our mothers, aunts, or grandmothers, we can still find out about friendship from the women who are most prominent in our lives now. The following pages are filled with real stories that capture the elements needed for friendships worth keeping for the rest of our lives.

Many women told us that among all the different relationships of which they were a part, the bonds with their girlfriends were extraordinary in their strength, flexibility, and durability. While we agree that many extraordinary tales of friendship are included here for you to enjoy, at the same time, the relationships underlying these tales are not unusual or uncommon. To the contrary—we, the authors, frequently express to each other our amazement at the stories which come from women everywhere. When we ask women to tell us about their friendships, the first response is usually, "Oh, I can't really think of any stories of our friendship," or something similar. But after talking for a few minutes, we will hear an impressive tale of loyalty, support, and love. Almost every woman experiences and appreciates these bonds, but may not have yet recognized the strength derived from these relationships. Fortunately, solid friendships between women abound.

Friends worth keeping forever often surprise us with their devotion, their laughter, and their affection. We often heard sentiments such as this one from Dena, from Rhode Island: "My girlfriends have far exceeded the expectations of friendship, and I thank God daily for blessing me with their love." We are proud to be able to participate in this celebration of girlfriends, and to honor relationships that transcend culture, location, and time.

Connecting

With friends who keep each other for life, we see a strong sense of connection. It is evident in the way women view their initial meeting — they feel they were meant to be friends and describe an instantaneous connection, parallel life paths, or even an initial dislike which sparked a curiosity with each other. Similarly, those friends come to recognize and acknowledge that connection through rituals and traditions, ways in which we emphasize the importance of the bond. Finally, girlfriends for life see each other in their futures, imagining their old age together and anticipating the fun to come.

We Were Meant to Be Friends

I've never been much of a religious person, but I've talked to God when times have been tough. I truly believe that God's answer was Cyndi. I wouldn't be anywhere close to where I am now if Cyndi hadn't come into my life.
I thank God every day for her.

—LESLI R. PONCHER-MILLER

"I think we were supposed to meet." "She came along just at the right time." "I don't know what I would have done if she had not turned up in my life."

A sense of destiny about meeting, a belief that the friendship was meant to be, was a common thread in the letters we received from women giving written tribute to their girlfriend relationships. Sometimes described as a sense of intuition or feeling safe and understood, many women described having an instantaneous connection to women they had just met.

Early Recognition

An immediate bond can form at an early age, as Tara, now seventeen, described in her letter about her good friend Emily: "The first time we actually met was in first grade, but we were destined for friendship long before that. Before I started first grade, I looked at the pictures of the other kindergarten classes, which were going to be combined with mine the following year. I started to draw mustaches on all of their faces. When I got to Emily, I just circled her several times, and then continued to draw mustaches on everyone else. I guess I liked the way she looked! When we were put in the same first grade class, it all kicked off. We took dancing lessons together, piano lessons, played on the same soccer team, and even liked the same boy. Much to her dismay, he liked me. We were also in the same second grade class and we continued to do everything together. Where there was Emily, there was Tara. And vice versa."

The common understanding and connection felt in the first moments of acquaintance often signify an understanding that lasts throughout the friendship. That understanding may show itself in the shared love of an activity. Tara and Emily's story is especially revealing in the way that women often relate to each other. Whether we're playing soccer as little girls, going to dances together as teenagers, or going on shopping sprees as adults, underneath the surface activity a deep bond is being forged. The actual activity is quite secondary, as women use these moments to share personal feelings, private longings, and their true essence with each other. The key element in creating this bond is recognizing a friendly face in a crowd of strangers.

Vanessa also remembers feeling that instant connection with her friend Melissa when starting high school: "I moved to Los Angeles when I was starting the ninth grade, and had lived there for only two weeks when I met Melissa at a church youth group meeting. During the first conversation we had, one of us said, 'So where have you been all my life?' We were best friends immediately.

"Even though we went to different high schools and eventually different colleges, we've lived in different states and have very different interests, we have never lost contact. When I go visit her, she drops everything to be with me, and I do the same. She came up to Portland to visit me over the summer, and everything stopped. There were two days of Melissa. And even though we're adults now, we still giggle about inside jokes we've had since the ninth grade."

Vanessa identified her lifelong girlfriend in those first scary weeks of moving to a new city and starting high school, and that sense of "knowing" one another would remain a key element throughout their friendship. It was as if she just knew that Melissa would provide a haven of familiarity in an otherwise unsettling time, and Melissa did. Vanessa was able to rely on the comfort of having someone understand her from the first instant of their meeting.

Drawn Together by a Common Love

You do not have to be starting school to meet a lifelong friend nor do you both have to be the same age. A common love can bring two women together, and provide a basis to discover a deeper connection. Two such friends met when one was forty and the other was eighty, drawn together by the fact that they both spoke French and shared a love for cats, facts which were apparent in their first five minutes of acquaintance. Marlene wrote us, "One Halloween I went to the mall to buy some decorations. I noticed some stationery packets and especially liked the ones with cats on them. I decided they would make nice Christmas gifts. I was picking out all the ones with cat motifs when I glanced at the gray-haired woman standing next to me, who looked back at me and said, with a distinctive French accent, 'I've had a cat for sixteen years.' I asked if she wanted any of the stationery, since

I was about to buy all of the ones with cats on them, and she declined. She told me she once took care of a woman who used to say to her, 'Ceux qui n'aiment pas les chats ne les connaissent pas' (Those who do not like cats, do not know them).

"What a joy it was for me to meet someone who spoke French, as I teach French at the local university. I responded to her in French, which of course surprised her, and we talked as we shopped together and eventually made our way to the cashier. Amazingly enough, the cashier, named Monique, was a former French student of mine, and the three of us had the most wonderful time conversing together.

"She told me her name was Gertrude, and that she was twice my age (I being forty and she eighty years of age). She also told me she'd read something very profound that day, and I wrote it down on the only piece of paper I had, which was the receipt from the store. The saying was, 'Le bonheur, c'est le moment quand il n'y a pas de chagrin' (Happiness is the moment when there are no worries).

"We have been in touch since that first meeting. I believe that our paths crossed because of fate, drawn together by our willingness to recognize a friend when first we meet."

Some friends meet while participating in their favorite activities, such as playing tennis, volunteering to help at a community theater, or attending painting classes. Their common interest may be the fateful element which brings them together. Other women told us that the fact that they had made a life decision at approximately the same time was the catalyst for their lifetime friendship. For example, a number of women told us about friendships that began when they first became mothers, and had child-rearing challenges in common. Cheri wrote us about her "special group of four girlfriends, which started fifteen years ago and is still going strong. Judy, Jeanette, Arlene, Nancy and I met while teaching at the same school, and, amazingly enough, we were all pregnant at the same time. We shared every joy and pain of pregnancy and delivered happy, healthy babies. We decided to meet every month to let our babies play together and to discuss our worries about being first-time moms.

"Our children have grown up together and get along like brothers and sisters. We continue to meet once a month. Together we've gone from teething, potty training, and the terrible twos and are now facing the teenage years. We know, with the help of each other, we will get through these years, too.

"Even though we no longer work at the same school, we're closer than ever. We consider each other more than friends—we are sisters. We've shared many happy times as well as sad ones. We've gone through operations, the loss of loved ones, and now my girl-friends are helping me through my fight with cancer. They are always there for me when I need them. I feel thankful for my special friends."

In some cases, fate deals two women a similar hand, and they build on that connection by making similar life choices. Tanya wrote about meeting Christine, her lifelong friend, when she was only six months old and Christine was one year old: "It all began at the community pool, when our mothers met and began chatting. Christine and I were just babies. I was in need of a hat for my bald head and was given Christine's. This is the object that brought us together, in a way. We still have the hat and plan to pass it back and forth for our own children to wear.

"We have amazing characteristics in common. Our fathers are both German, and the order and ages of our siblings are the same, with Christine and I being the youngest. She and I went to the same elementary school, junior high school, and high school, where we doubled dated at our high school proms.

"We even roomed together our first year of college, and even though we went to separate colleges after that first year, we both went on to graduate school to become psychotherapists, working primarily with children. Within two months of each other, we became engaged to men who work in finance, and we were married within three months of each other. We kept our maiden names, both long names beginning with the letter *K*.

"Our memories are so abundant and rich; our influence on each other has been profound. We have argued with teachers on each other's behalf, forged parents' signatures in the name of friendship, told each other's ex-boyfriends what louses they were, held hands while walking through unfamiliar hallways, and still laugh at the part in the movie no one else finds funny. The parallel events that have shaped our lives are the outside evidence of the magical bond we know we have inside, on a deeper level."

A Meeting of Opposites

Sometimes the meant-to-be quality of a friendship is not apparent to the women involved, but to those observing. Tracey told us how she nearly overlooked the friendship that was possible with Anna Maria, if it hadn't been for Flo, Anna Maria's mother. "Anna Maria and I met on our first day at college in Atlanta. The dorms were converted apartments. There were three bedrooms, two bathrooms and six young women. Anna Maria is a five-foot, eight-inch New Jersey Italian; I am five-foot, three-inches and Southern Irish and, at that time, wasn't quite out of my punk rock stage. We looked like Mutt & Jeff together.

"Flo, Anna Maria's mother, turned prophetic on us and told us that, of the six roommates, Anna Maria and I would be the best friends. We looked at each other, then gave her a you-have-*got*-to-be-kidding look. However, the difficulties and challenges of being away from home for the first time brought us together. That was in 1987, and Flo still reminds us at every opportunity that she was right."

Sometimes we are drawn to friends because of our similarities, like Tanya and Christine, or despite our differences, like Anna Maria and Tracey. Opposites can definitely attract, as we sometimes seek in another person what might be less developed in ourselves—a shy girl may be attracted to the outgoing personality of a schoolmate or a visionary may find herself feeling more "grounded" by the down-to-earth outlook of a friend. Peggy, describing her strong bond with Rae Lynn, which has spanned four decades, wrote, "Rae Lynn's bubbly, crazy personality was a counterbalance to my serious, responsible demeanor. We became instant, inseparable friends. Throughout junior high school, we kept a running notebook exchange, using secret code names 'Kooky' and 'Witty,' in which we espoused our opinions on every topic from which boy had the coolest blue eyes to which girl had the tackiest tight skirt to which teacher was the lamest. How I wish we still had those notebooks!

"Rae Lynn and her family moved during our sophomore year in high school. To this day, my list of 'devastating experiences' includes the moment I heard she was leaving. I felt as though half of me left with her. Although we have remained each other's oldest and dearest friends, time and circumstances separate us. I send her long, detailed letters about my family and my job. She has changed husbands, jobs, states, and even her name—it's Rachael now. But to me, she's still Rae Lynn."

A Rough Spot

Other long-lasting friendships are noteworthy by the negative note on which their relationship began. Sometimes we bristle toward one another at first, even though underneath our differences beats the heart of a true friend. From what we heard from women everywhere, it doesn't seem to matter to the life of the friendship whether that first fateful connection was a positive or negative one—so long as it was memorable! Many friends who now believe they were meant to be together, told us about their initial dislike for each other. Debbie relayed to us, "My best friend, Susan, and I are forty-four years old and have been friends for thirty years; however, our friendship did not have an auspicious beginning. We were thrown together in our seventh-grade homeroom. I hated her from the moment she opened her mouth! She was loud, obnoxious, funny—the proverbial class clown—all the things I was not. We were complete opposites in every way; but all those traits I hated in her, I also admired. She exuded confidence, which I sorely lacked, and seemed to draw people to her like a magnet.

"At the end of the year, I was involved with my first boyfriend, and he wanted to buy me a ring. His allowance wasn't much, so he took up a collection (imagine!) from his classmates. Of course, Susan was not a contributor. Thank goodness, or I'd have to forever hear about how she had a vested interest in my jewelry!

"During the summer, my boyfriend and I broke up, and when school began in the fall, guess who he asked to go with him? I really hated her then! It wasn't until after they broke up that we became friends, because now we had something in common—the same ex-boyfriend. Yet, it was not until our freshman year in high school, when we shared a locker, that we became *best* friends and remain so to this day." Just as a pearl is formed from an irritating piece of sand in an oyster, precious friendships may develop after an annoying beginning. From a rocky start in a shared homeroom, to bonding over a shared boyfriend (or ex-boyfriend), Debbie and Susan learned they were meant to be friends.

Similarly, Glori told us this story about when she met her best friend, Kim: "Six months before I met Kim, I had moved from California to my future husband's home town in the Midwest. I had a job at a downtown clothing store, checking in shipments. When I was asked to become a salesperson, this woman named Kim, who had also just moved to town to be with her boyfriend, took my old job. I thought she was very funny, but I also thought she was not taking her job seriously enough, and that annoyed me. I am very finicky about how I do things, and I now know that Kim thought I was something of a dragon lady. It wasn't until I took her out to lunch about a month or two later, that she started thinking we could be friends.

"It is kind of ironic that she thought I was humorless at first, because that was twenty years ago, and now we spend a lot of our time together in laughter. In fact, a couple of years ago, we were in a class together and always making trouble. We misbehave so similarly, although in all other things we are very different. I still am more finicky, and she is more casual. Physically, she is dark-complected, about ten inches taller than I am, and always looking for extra-long pants, and I am very fair skinned with blond hair, and shop in the children's department for my clothes. As we were cutting up in this class together, a woman turned to us and said, 'Are you two twins?' We just looked at each other and laughed, but she was serious. I guess we are soul mates in making trouble."

Friendship Meant to Endure

Some relationships move through the years without any break in contact. However, some friends grow apart through life's transitions. We can see the destiny in these friendships when these friends reconnect later in life to reclaim a friendship meant to endure. We received one letter from two friends, Alice and Julie, who found each other after losing touch for more than fifteen years. In the newsletter they create together they recently published their story, part of which is included here: "In 1960, two girls, Alice and Julie, met in second grade in southern New Jersey. They shared school, church, Brownies, and free time, and Alice's family was a great support to Julie's mother when Julie's father died suddenly. At the end of fifth grade, Alice's family moved to Massachusetts. The girls tried to stay in contact through letters. Julie wrote delightful letters, but Alice hated writing and couldn't think of anything to say. They lost touch.

"By 1982 the girls had grown up, married, and relocated to the Midwest: Julie to Illinois, and Alice to Wisconsin. Knowing that her friend was in Wisconsin, one day Julie sat down with that state's phone book and proceeded to track down her old friend. They met for the first time in many years at a Milwaukee restaurant, carrying their photo albums to help them get caught up. They discovered that their careers had both included teaching, Alice at first and Julie after several other careers. Julie had lived for some time in Italy, while Alice had adventured in this country. The women continued to meet on occasion, and their teenage children got to know each other.

"In 1996, Alice, frustrated by the media's tired old messages to teenage girls, decided to send her own more healthy messages to them. She contacted Julie and together they developed a newsletter for teenage girls called *Sights*. Now in daily contact through e-mail, they share thoughts and problems and experiences in their personal, professional, and volunteer lives, as well as share the creation of the newsletter. They marvel at the twists their lives have taken and the many pleasures of their friendship renewed. They leave you with this thought: Life is exciting, unpredictable, and everything else you make it!"

Like Alice and Julie, Jorja told us about rediscovering a friend after losing track of her for years: "About a year ago, I happened to be passing the time one evening watching the skaters at an outdoor ice rink in Oregon. The rink had just opened after much community effort and fund-raising. I noticed and proceeded to read a plaque which had been placed near the rink that listed all the contributors. On the very last line of the plaque I read the name 'Stephanie Soares Pump.' I had to do a doubletake.

"I grew up on the north shore of the island of Oahu in what was, in the mid-fifties, the Territory of Hawaii. Stephanie Soares was my very best friend. After my family moved to the mainland, we continued to write for a few years but lost touch during our high school years. Imagine my surprise at finding her after nearly forty years, with her living so close to me! Fortunately for me, Stephanie kept her maiden name as her middle name." Who would have guessed that by using her maiden name, Stephanie would have made it possible for Jorja to locate her and give them the chance to pick up their friendship where they left off so many years ago. Perhaps they would have found each other eventually, as they were again living in the same community. Whatever the case, their re-connection allowed them to continue their friendship.

Carmen, one of the authors of this book, was especially pleased when she heard from two old friends,

Melissa and Donna, who had gotten together for a visit with each other, and out of that visit, became "accidentally" reconnected with Carmen. Melissa wrote, "I got in touch with Donna because I was going through a particularly tough time in my life. I had quit my job as a management assistant after working for many years. The circumstances around my leaving were very unfortunate, and consequently, I felt lost and alone, and my confidence was shaken.

"The following week, I flew to Los Angeles to visit my best friend, Donna. I knew that somehow seeing her would help me make sense of my decision and was sure that she would help me regain some of my self-esteem. We literally grew up together in every sense of the word. We were in Brownies, Girl Scouts, went to the same schools, did all of the things that girls do together and eventually even married brothers. Donna and I both have children, so we are always sharing stories about our kids. We cried our eyes out when our sons left for the service and I couldn't wait to tell her I was going to be a grandma! To say that we shared 'the times of our lives' is truly an understatement. She has always been there for me, even though sometimes years will go by without seeing each other. We share a bond with one another that is so strong that many times one of us has picked up the phone and called the other, only to hear her say, 'I was just going to call you!'

"During our visit, we laughed, cried, reminisced about the good old days, looked at old pictures, year-books, drove around town (Donna still lives in the town in which we grew up) and talked for what seemed like forever. Somehow things just seemed better when I was 'home' with Donna. Not only did I have my share of problems, but Donna was also going through her own difficult times. The timing of seeing each other was incredible, being there for each other was something I'll never forget.

"On one of our outings, we ran by a book store to hunt down those books on 'stuff' that only women go through. While walking down the aisle, I remembered that Donna's birthday was approaching and I wanted to get her something special. I picked up only one book from the shelf—your book *girlfriends*. As I glanced through the book, I decided that this was the perfect gift, as it expressed my feelings at having such a friend. When I turned the book over and read the back cover, the hair on my neck must have stood straight up. I realized that one of the authors of the book was Carmen. Donna and I had gone to high school with her.

"As I grabbed a birthday card and rushed to the counter, I kept looking at Carmen's picture thinking, 'Boy, this is weird.' Imagine celebrating our girlfriend bond with a book written by a girlfriend we had both known years ago. Somehow I managed to keep the book and my story a secret until I got home. I asked Donna's daughter to give her mom my gift on her birthday.

"On her birthday, I called Donna and told her the story about the book. Needless to say, she was stunned and surprised! She agreed that life definitely takes some peculiar turns and that things like this happen for a reason. We were there for each other, and after all, isn't that what friendship is all about?"

Friends often rediscover each other in these seemingly accidental ways, but occasionally they need to meet up more than once. Friends may keep turning up in our lives until we are ready to recognize them as the valuable relationships they are meant to be. Tracey wrote to us about her friend Michelle, "My friendship with Michelle started off a little slow. My roommate, Olivia, and Michelle bonded immediately, and I have to admit I was a little jealous of this new friendship. Olivia really wanted us all to be friends so Michelle and I went to a rock concert together, trying to bond and keep Olivia from being stuck in the middle. The concert was horrible, but it was a beginning. Gradually, we discovered what Olivia loved so much about each of us."

Once Tracey and Michelle started talking with one another, they found their life experiences so uncannily parallel that it seems they could not have avoided building a lifelong friendship, even if they had tried!

Tracey continued: "As we got to know each other better, we discovered some bizarre parallels. We found out that when we were nine years old, we took gymnastics at the same gym. We don't remember each other but were probably in the same class. Then, we worked at the same department store at the same time but in different departments. We never met. After that, we attended the same college, pursued the same major, and were in the same classes. We still didn't notice each other. It took Olivia bringing her into my life before I recognized one of my best friends.

"Now we are called The Wonder Twins because we are so much alike. We frightened Olivia and a waitress one afternoon. Michelle and I were sitting across from each other and Olivia was sitting next to me. The waitress brought our drinks and set them in front of us. Michelle and I were mirror images as we squeezed the lemon into the tea, poked it down with the spoon, set the spoon down, took a sip, and set the glass down on the opposite side from where the waitress had put it. All perfectly synchronized. To this day, we finish each other's sentences, come up with really bizarre thoughts at the same time and beat everybody at Pictionary™. What would I do without her?"

Tracey and Michelle did not stand a chance—it seems that their destinies pushed them together until they became friends. Linda told us how a now-close friend kept appearing in her life: "When I was twenty-six, I went to a party in Michigan for a friend of mine from the university. There, I ran into a woman, Mary, whom I immediately recognized as someone that I had gone to elementary school with but only knew during the third and fourth grades. My family had moved away from the area when I went to the fifth grade, as did hers. She was shocked that I remembered her and that I could even recognize her, but to me, she looked the same as when I had known her.

"We started talking and I instantly felt a closeness to her. I was so happy that I ran into her. It brought back memories of childhood that one should never lose. I called her, and we had lunch shortly thereafter. Unfortunately, I moved to California for graduate school that following summer, and she moved to a new home. We both had so much going on in our lives.

"Two years passed, and I had not contacted her but thought about her often. Luckily, fate brought us together again. I saw her at a Christmas party in Michigan the following year, to which she almost did not go. We connected so well that it felt like I had never even left. It was so easy to talk to her, and we have so much in common. Our conversation never felt odd, and there was so much to talk about. I wish that we had not lost so much time, but I am thankful that we were meant to find each other again. She has appeared at a time in my life when I really need someone like her. She understands things that even some of my other dearest and closest friends do not, because she and I are at the same point in our lives and share common goals. We are now planning a vacation together, and I'm sure that I will never lose contact with her again. She truly is special because she brings back a feeling of familiarity and we always treasure things from our past."

Whether a friendship begins instantly at first meeting or takes time to grow, looking back on how we first met can generate enormous feelings of gratitude for the development of the friendship and leave us with a sense of destiny and purpose. What would our lives have been like without these relationships, these women who came into our lives at just the right moment.

Many times we feel that our friends are sent to us from heaven. We do not often pause in our busy days to reflect on the "meant to be" quality of our relationships with other women. How do you say thank you to someone for being your friend? We can start by just saying it. When we read the stories, included here, we are reminded of the power of these relationships. Perhaps these stories will inspire all of us to make a call or send a letter to one or more of our closest friends, saying, "Thank you for coming into my life. It wouldn't have been the same without you."

Rituals That Bind

We have spent New Year's Eve together for about thirty years, sometimes with many other people, sometimes with just a few. I just think it is something we wouldn't ever want to give up.

—JANE CARVER

Women friends who stay an important part of each other's lives often find themselves "reserving" a particular activity for their friendship. As one woman told us, "My friend and I wouldn't think of seeing a new Mel Gibson movie without each other. It's practically a religious experience as we worship at The Altar of Mel. While it's all in fun, it is also reassuring to me that we have this tradition—no matter how busy we are, we both know we are going to get together on these occasions."

Regularly sharing an activity, creating a tradition, or developing a ritual unique to a friendship not only provides a meaningful moment, but is also a way of celebrating and strengthening the friendship bond. When we wrote our first book about women's friendship, we knew little about how many wild, fun, and irreverent ways women recognize and celebrate their connection with each other. We discovered that sometimes the celebrations are one-time events, while others are long-standing traditions, some are serious, some are raucous, but all are executed with respect for their significance in the girlfriend relationship.

A Simple Gesture,
A Lifelong Tradition

Traditions take time to develop, and can start with a small gesture. Dode sent us a letter describing how an act of kindness started a tradition she and her close friend, Becki, have maintained for over two decades. She wrote, "Becki and I met in 1964 and always kept in touch. I thought she was really stuckup. Little did I know that underneath that reservoir of impeccable manners was a person of shyness and kindness.

"One day at work, a particularly trying day, Becki dropped by, unannounced, to say hi and also to bring me a gift: a small decorative can filled with candy. I can't tell you how that small gesture helped me get through the day. It was a note of cheer that I will always remember. When the can was empty, instead of pushing it in the corner of a closet or tossing it, I decided to fill it with something small and return it—hence the launching of the Friendship Can and a deeper level to our friendship. Since that time in 1978, whoever has the can returns it with something—it can be stamps or a pair of bobby socks or whatever we think the other will like. If the particular item doesn't fit in the can, we make sure the can is enclosed with the item. There isn't any set pattern or time limit. Our Friendship Can is a part of our thirty-plus years of togetherness, and it will continue to be a part of the rest of our lives."

As a simple gesture can be the basis for a tradition, so can a shared interest. Jean told us this story of a tradition which arose from an enjoyment of shopping she shared with Constance, whom she first met working in a neonatal intensive care unit. Jean wrote, "Constance was twenty-five at the time, and I was a little older—thirty-seven to be exact. You would think we would be closer in age for such a close bond; nevertheless, we've been best of friends for twelve years now, and I'm sure we'll be friends through eternity.

"One thing we treasure, just for the two of us, is our shopping. The second year into our friendship, we started taking a special Christmas shopping trip, not just for a day but for two to three days, in different states and even different countries. On these trips, we have plenty of sharing time and have created wonderful memories. We are fortunate to have supportive husbands who understand the importance of our trips. This year marks our ninth trip, with next year's trip a special surprise to include the guys, since they tease us about getting their turn! It will be my thirtieth wedding anniversary and Constance will be celebrating her tenth.

"We keep journals of our times together and let each other read them. How much fun it is to share what the other has remembered. One trip Connie had just given birth to her second son and was nursing; however, that didn't stop us—we took a cooler and she pumped when necessary and the ounces were recorded in my journal."

Making the Effort

Rather than making a ritual for creating memories, as Jean and Constance have done, it is easy to let time slip by as we get caught up in the demands of daily living. Some friends have discovered that if they don't schedule ahead and make time to get together, too many weeks, months, and years pass before they are together again. Mandy told us about a tradition which guarantees her group of friends will see each other every year: "The year 1997 marked the eighth anniversary for what my friends and I call 'Little Angels.' Heather, Katie, Myra, Liesel, Leah, Julie, Sandy, and I gather over Thanksgiving weekend, usually at Katie's, to bake cookies.

"After the cookies are made, we have a slumber party and watch movies, pig out, and, after we were old enough, celebrate with some drinks. We then each write down our names and something little we might like to receive as a gift and each of us draws a name. Everyone then has until Christmas to get that special gift. Around Christmas time, we get together again to exchange gifts and have another slumber party. This tradition even endured when Katie was in Germany, as we sent her a box of cookies. We now live in many different cities — New York, Dallas, Pittsburgh, Washington D.C., Florida, and Hollidaysburg, Pennsylvania — and though we can't get together as often as we would like, we will always be Little Angels. My friends have always been a source of strength and comfort to me, and I love and miss them dearly. I can't wait to see them all again."

Commitment and planning are necessary ingredients to creating rituals. As our lives change, however, a commitment to carrying out our girlfriend traditions may require that our traditions change as well. Rose and her girlfriends go on an annual outing that has evolved to accommodate her personal circumstances: "Last year several of my friends and I went on a camping trip to celebrate our birthdays (three of the girlfriends have birthdays around the same time). We all love the outdoors, and we had a pretty rugged trip — hiking tough trails, swimming, jumping off huge boulders.

"This year we celebrated our birthdays again with a camping trip, but this time I was pregnant, so our camping trip changed significantly. One of the women's fathers drove his camper to a campsite at a national park, and we girls went alone to stay in it. We hardly left the camper all weekend! One of us brought lasagna, so all we had to do was put it in the oven to cook.

Everyone was so accommodating — every decision was left to me — Rose, 'do you want to take the easy trail or the hard trail?' 'Do you feel like eating now or do you want to wait?' 'Here, Rose, take the bed, we will sleep on the floor.' It couldn't compare in hardiness to the trip we had taken the first year, but I expect that we will get back to it when we are together again — and I am not pregnant." The activity, or how strenuous it might have been, did not matter — Rose and her gal pals were acutely aware of the importance of simply spending time together. If these girlfriends had not adjusted their tradition to take Rose's circumstances into account, Rose probably would not have been there to participate in the outing. Doubtless, as her child grows, the camping will change again and again.

At the other end of the child-rearing process, women whose children have grown told us that over the years their traditions with their girlfriends have grown more elaborate. Cheri and her friends, women who all met teaching at the same school and then raised their children together, told us how their traditional activities have gotten more luxurious: "Our get-togethers that started with simple cookies and coffee have developed into lavish meals and a yearly, full-day progressive meal for Christmas. Now that our children are growing up, we have more opportunities to spend time together. We are looking forward to going out for lunches, shopping trips, and visiting other places. We know that whatever the future holds, we will be there for each other."

Sometimes, losing a girlfriend can make women realize how much they appreciate the girlfriends they do have and can be the impetus to start a tradition. When Lois's friend, Carolyn, died suddenly and un-expectedly in her early forties, Lois and four mutual girlfriends decided to start keeping a journal chroni-cling all of the major events in their lives. They pass the book to the next girlfriend on the occasion of each of their birthdays. Lois wrote, "After the loss of Carolyn, we began to treasure our friendship more, and so, for sixteen years, four of my best women friends and I have met for each others' birthdays.

"For me, this has become one place where I can touch base with the past and be able to integrate the present. As time goes on, the ritual becomes more and more important not because we need to celebrate another birthday, but because we need to sit with each other and laugh and cry about the latest events in each other's lives. We've chronicled births, deaths, sicknesses, weddings, and tears of joy and sadness. Three of us have divorced, two are widowed (one widowed twice), two have had cancer, one has had a miscarriage, and one has lost a child. Two were married, two children were born, and five grandchildren were born. In addition to recording the years' events in the journal, we share our hopes, fears, angers, expectations, and aspirations. We've all grown from the process. Through our shared book the message is clear, we all value having each other to share our joys and burdens with."

Few of us have ample time to contemplate what is actually happening in our lives and the effects of these events. As Lois illustrates, her friendship circle gives each of the women the time to share their experiences, to talk about the meaning of those experiences, and to be heard and affirmed by those who really care about them. Through her death, Carolyn gave her friends a gift—the gift of reminding them that life is short, that we can lose a friend unexpectedly, and that we need to make room in our lives to show our appreciation for the people who matter to us.

I Value You

Showing appreciation is a central component of friendships that last. Linda remembers how a girlfriend created a one-time ritual for showing her friends what they meant to her. Linda wrote that when her friend turned fifty, she "had a big party in a private room at a restaurant. She called each person to stand up in the front and she told everyone how she met them and what they meant to her. Then we had a slumber party with movies, games, and other girl stuff."

The more we let our girlfriends know how much they are valued, the stronger our friendships grow. Appreciation can be shown in a variety of ways. Sometimes a symbolic tribute can be a way of celebrating female relationships. As Cynthia explained to us: "My home is filled with items I've received from my girlfriends, as well as from my grandmother, aunt, and mother, such as blankets, photos, books, cups, and so on. One day I thought of a creative project idea that was motivated by love and admiration of my important women connections.

"While browsing through the local thrift store, I found a night stand for five dollars—a seventies classic, decoupage green with brass hardware. I painted the table white and trimmed it in gold. With gold and silver paint pens, I wrote the names of the women in my life. I started with names of women who are no longer on this earth—great names they were, too: Inga, Inez, Carol, and Alma. As I started to write, and draw random swirls, hearts, and squiggles, I realized that the cycle of love and support from women continues, and that I'm now drawing strength from the women who are still present: Sonja, Julie, and Debra. Most important, I realized that I am passing on lessons and wisdom to young women like Sade, who is from the younger generation. So, the table carries many names, and I continue to add women from the past, the present, and the future. It is the table of the 'women in my life,' and almost seems to emanate their collective spirit. It sits alongside my bed, and often, before falling asleep, I touch it lightly, almost unconsciously, and take a moment to be thankful for these precious women."

The creation of traditions, rituals, and symbols shows that we have made a permanent place for our friends in our lives and acknowledges the contribution those friends make to the quality of our experience. They ground us, letting us know that we are still there for each other. Traditions or rituals are also the outward manifestation of feelings of appreciation. If we take the time to do something with a friend or let her know how we feel about her, we are celebrating the importance of the friendship in our lives. Friendships that are honored by a symbol, or a regularly scheduled celebration are more likely to survive than those in which long periods of time pass without acknowledgment. Once we indicate how important a girlfriend is to us, we strengthen the bond and invigorate the relationship itself.

We Are Friends with a Future

I am grateful for a friend who knows without being told, does without asking, and gives without taking. I am grateful for someone who understands when the whole world doesn't. I am joyous in anticipation of what the next twenty years hold in store for me and my best friend.

—JUDY LANE

No matter where we are in our life's journey, we all have a future to imagine. Often we can tell who our best girlfriends are by whether we see them in our future plans. Whether it's envisioning a road trip with our best pal to Graceland next year or living together in our old age, we know that our exceptional girlfriends will be in our lives in some way. Amy wrote about her best friend Daari: "When we were in high school, a teacher told us for some reason that our friendship would never last. We are now seniors in college and the test of time has proven that teacher wrong. We attend different schools and don't get to see each other as often as we would like. However, we both understand that even though we have different lives now, it doesn't threaten our relationship. She is my best friend and always will be. We have plans for an apartment after college and joke about us being ninety years old, sitting in our rocking chairs gossiping away."

Sharing in the Next Generation

Vickie and Erika, another pair of friends, look to the future with the hope that the bond they've forged will withstand the pressures of time, especially the challenges of motherhood. Vickie, a young mother, has faith that their friendship will endure because their connection to each other has already been tested and found true. "We both know our friendship will grow more and more no matter what life deals us. We've already proven that to each other. I look forward to the day when Erika weds and becomes a mom for the first time like I have. I know we're going to share so much of our lives together as the years go by."

In the meantime, Erika may become an auntie to Vickie's children. Often women keep each other in their lives by making each other part of their respective families. A woman who has children often hopes that her girlfriend will be an auntie to her children, a trusted adult to whom their children can go to when they cannot go to mom and dad. Including our friends in the task of raising our offspring strengthens those bonds of friendship in an irreversible way.

Sherry, in her early fifties, told this story about how her friend, Julie, stepped in during a tumultuous time in Sherry's life and not only helped raise Sherry's children, but strengthened the friendship bond with Sherry. She said, "We met in high school. Both our last names started with 'Co,' so we sat next to each other in homeroom all four years, but other than being in those classes together, we never did anything else together. We graduated, and both became hippies (it was the sixties). One day, a third friend said to me, 'I want you to come over to my friends' house, they have a new baby.' So I went to visit and she turned out to be that woman I sat next to in high school. We were so surprised, we couldn't believe it.

"When I had my son Jay, she and I were the only two people in our circle who had children. We ended up raising our children together. We were very good friends, and our children became good friends as well, always going to visit each other on vacation when we lived in different towns.

"Then my first husband and I split up, and I got involved with Mike, who I've now been married to for ten years. Mike could not be more different from my ex-husband, and my new life could not be more different than my ex-life. Mike was, and still is, a teacher and seemed more conservative. When my friends met Mike, they thought he was this straight elementary school teacher. So I didn't know what would happen with my friends. But Julie didn't skip a beat at all.

"She completely accepted Mike. She also made herself available to my kids a lot, so that there was another stabilizing force in their lives. She supported my decision to marry Mike and made sure that my family was going to be okay. Together, we have a very strong extended family. I understand I wasn't the only person who raised my children — she was very important in my kids' lives. Our sons have stayed close, too — they lived together for several years."

Julie has shown that Sherry can always count on her. She made sure she stayed in Sherry's life, even after it had completely changed. Sherry laughed as she illustrated this point with another story: "Julie and I always had spent New Year's Eve together. The first New Year's Eve that Mike and I were together, we were off in our own little world. Julie just came to the house, and pounded on the door at 11:30 P.M., and said, 'It's New Year's Eve, you guys! You think you are leaving me out of it? I'm here!'"

Similarly, Rose, Gloria, and Alona have every intention of staying in each other's lives — as mothers and as friends. Rose, who is six months pregnant, is looking forward to raising her children with her friends: "Now that I am going to have a child and Gloria just had one, our kids will be just months apart. One of my old friends, Alona, just had a baby last April, so our babies are a year apart. What I see now is us building our future with our kids together.

"Gloria and her husband, Steve, are already saying things like 'If the kids want to go camping together, they are going to have to go with Aunt Rose and Uncle Brad, because we don't do camping. Anything having to do with outdoor activities, that is what Rose and Brad are there for!' We also talk about renting a villa in Italy when the kids are older. That is the sort of thing we can all do together."

Shared lifestyles and values will keep many friends together far into the future. Leyza told us: "My best friend, Jan, and I have each decided not to have children. There's a silent understanding about the future in light of the fact that we know we will never be tied down with kids or a life of domesticity. She and I are best pals—we travel all over the world together. We take trips to New York, Miami, Europe, and Mexico; our incredible bond and similar interests and tastes enable us to have fun doing anything and everything from shopping and working out to seeing art exhibits and going dancing.

"The two of us call each other 'Fruit,' so when we go out on the town (whatever the city), we describe it as 'Fruit and Fruit go out.' We always say, 'When we are eighty, will we still be making scenes at the Royalton Hotel? Are we still going to be able to get into the hottest dance clubs in New York? Jan is really tall and blonde with great legs and always says, 'Well, Fruit, the legs are the last to go!' So, we're confident we will still be causing trouble (and getting past the velvet ropes) even when we're old. It is a neat thing for both of us to know that we have the same philosophy about adventure and freedom. It's not that we don't value family, but we just treasure our independence so much. That is partly what creates the unique bond between us, to be best friends, and know that we'll be 'Fruit and Fruit' forever."

Thinking Long-Term

Looking beyond one's immediate circumstances enables friends to see each other in their futures. Life never stays the same! Rose talks about how she anticipates that some friends may drift away a bit as she busies herself with motherhood, but that she knows that eventually her circumstances will change again: "You can think long term if you have something that you like to do together. Yes, I will have kids, and go through this phase of my life with family vacations and so forth, but I also think I will want to go to Europe again. My husband, Brad, is not going to want to go, because he has been there so many times. So I am thinking, 'Well when the kids are older, I can go with my girlfriends.' I look past when the kids are young. Even though I say it is easy to drift from some of your friends when you have kids, as long as you stay in contact, you can pick up the friendship, and similar interests, later.

When thinking longterm, friendship does not require day-to-day contact to remain viable. Rose told us, "My husband heard me refer to one of my friends the other day whom I hadn't seen much in the last few years, and he asked me: 'Do you still consider her a good friend? You don't have that much in common anymore.' I said, 'Of course.' My friend, Sherrie, and I knew each other before we were married. I was in her wedding. After she started having a couple of kids, we sort of drifted apart, and then I moved to a different city. In fact, I didn't even tell her I was moving, it happened so fast. I called her up one day and said, 'Oh, I've been such a bad friend, Sherrie.' And she said 'Oh, I am too, I am really bad about calling.' And I said, 'No, no, no, you don't understand! I don't even live in the same city you live in anymore!' But she was fine with that; she didn't get upset about it, and we caught up about our husbands and our lives. So we had that period where we hadn't seen each other in years, and we would get together once in a while.

"But now that I am having kids, we e-mail and call each other and it has come full circle where we are talking again more often. It doesn't even matter that we haven't seen each other in years, because we still have the same connection. That to me is the sign of a true friendship, when you can not communicate for ages and you can go right back to where you were."

We agree. If one is able to relax and trust that we will be able to stay in one another's lives, then we probably will. But we have to be confident that shared memories and mutual affection will hold strong during periods of absence or decreased contact. We only have to remember that the bonds of friendship do not have to be tied too tightly for friends to stay friends.

This Is Going to Be Fun

As women look to the future and growing old together, many express a vision with a sense of security and joyful anticipation. Randi wrote us about her lifelong friendship with Carol, saying "I expect her to be as much a part of my future as she has been in my past. I envision our getting together and slowing down to a gentler pace. We may have more 'laugh lines' around our eyes, or a few more aches in our joints, but our friendship will be as healthy as ever."

In the past, a woman planning her senior years may have looked solely to family members. Today's woman, however, often include 'girlfriends' in those plans as well. Linda wrote us about how her close girlfriend "has a plan for our old age where all of us girlfriends who meet once a month will live together in an independent nursing-home setting. It will have one big kitchen where we can cook and share meals, but each of us will have separate rooms for ourselves. We haven't figured out yet if we're letting in the husbands! However, we've still got some time to iron out the details."

More and more girlfriend groups are planning ahead, as Mary Jo's letter illustrated: "My story is one of true friends committed to one another through three decades plus. Members of 'The Clan'—Lynda, Kathy, Atanda, and I—were inseparable growing up in a small town in northern California. Each one of our families lived on a different street parallel to each other. From the end of these streets, we would meet and all walk to school together through the Sierra Desert. If one of us wore brown corduroy pants, we all did. We were quite a force to be reckoned with. No one messed with us, so to speak.

"Eventually we moved to other states, but that didn't alter our determination to hold on to what would prove to be the most bonded friendships we know. We get together once or twice a year, more if possible, and always communicate in-between those times. We're looking forward to being friends all of our lives. One of our favorite fantasies is that, once we turn sixty, we'll go to Florida and be the *Golden Girls*."

No one can predict the future, but our determination to stay connected to each other, whether it is for the next year or the next fifty, gives us a vision for the future and joy for today. For now, the best we can do is appreciate those precious women we choose to be our girlfriends and plan that they will be with us always—aren't they forever in our hearts and minds anyway?

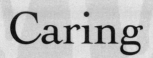

Caring

Girlfriends for life show they care for each other in a myriad of ways, with action that transcends mere affection. These women honor each other as individuals, respecting each others' differences, and encouraging and supporting the life choices of their friends, even when different from their own. Lifelong friends pay attention, knowing, sometimes uncannily, when the other needs help, and then step in when necessary to do what is needed. From sending a simple note to say "I'm thinking about you" to literally saving a girlfriend's life, the following stories pay tribute to the amazing ways women express their love to one another. Like us, you will be inspired, and maybe even astounded by the lengths women will go to tell their friends "I really care about you."

How Did You Know I Needed You?

*Friendship is not a matter of distance or frequency
but rather is a matter of the heart.*

—SANDRA F. RHEEM

We heard many times that a good girlfriend has very sensitive radar when it comes to her friend's welfare. We may get a call from a girlfriend just when we are feeling lonely or upset. Similarly, there are days when we may sense that our friend needs to hear from us. Who has not telephoned a friend and heard her say "I am so relieved you called!"? What is the source of that knowledge we have about each other? That intuition may simply stem from a heightened sense of consideration—our friend pays close attention to the details of our lives, and is aware of when we feel vulnerable, afraid, or stressed and need help. A friend for life knows us well, and with that knowledge, is cued into how we may be affected by the events of daily life. Her knowledge, and the use of it, expresses how she cares about us and our relationship.

She Knows Me So Well

Linda told us about her friend, Karen, who "loves to write poetry and is very reflective. Every once in a while, she will send me a little note, and it will have a tea bag in it. The note will say, 'I'm thinking of you. Have a cup of tea on me.' I seem to receive these treasures from her whenever I need them most—when I'm too busy focusing on what I'm trying to accomplish rather than the truly important things in life—family and friends."

Sometimes the slightest sign alerts our friends to the fact that we are struggling with a problem or need a caring set of ears. Many women mentioned that their closest friends only needed to hear the quality of their "hello" when they answered the phone to know when something is wrong. Jackie told us that no matter what her friend Sharon is going through, she always is able to recognize Jackie's state of mind: "Sharon will call me, and if something is bothering me, she hears it immediately in my voice. I will say 'hello' and she will respond with: 'What's wrong?' It is pretty amazing actually—she hears the slightest nuance. Even when she is calling to talk about something that is bothering her or a problem she needs to discuss with me, she always notices and always asks. It is so effective to talk to each other, too. Often she points out what is bothering me before I recognize it, and vice versa. Because we have had so many discussions, and remember so many details about each other's lives, we can usually get to the heart of each other's problems very quickly. We are each other's life historians."

Our ability to know what is going on with our girlfriends is usually a result of an intense awareness of her likes, dislikes, feelings, and general state. We are tuned in, because we care so much. Aimee described it this way: "There are times when we literally could be each other. We go shopping a lot together, and I can pinpoint what she'll buy before she even tries it on. She knows my favorites, and I hers. When we go out to eat, we can order for each other. I know her shoe size and the kind of makeup she uses. We always laugh at the same things, and our support for each other is unparalleled. She simply understands me, and I her."

Pure Empathy

Understanding what another woman needs may not require psychic ability—but it sometimes requires quick thinking and hard work. A lifelong girlfriend knows us well enough to realize when we need help, understands the kind of help we need, and has the gumption to roll up her sleeves and do what is needed.

We were touched by this story from Sylvia, who wrote to tell what her lovely friend Susan did for her when Sylvia and her family returned home to Lubbock, Texas, after an extended time away: "For the previous two years, we had been living in various countries of Europe. After my husband, daughters, and I staggered wearily from the plane and into the arms of friends and family, we were faced with the chore of getting furniture and household belongings out of storage and whipping our home into some sort of order before our children enrolled in school in just two weeks. Leaving the airport, the August sun beat on us from all directions. The airport terminal, the asphalt parking lot, and the hot metals of the cars radiated heat. Finally the four of us and our baggage were sorted among waiting cars and whisked to a welcome-home dinner.

"As we were having dinner, I was thinking about how I was not looking forward to renting a truck and wrestling furniture from a hot storage unit into our hot house. With doors wide open for the move, any attempt at air conditioning would, of course, be futile. My friend Susan then asked if we were going to see our house before retiring that night. Sighing, I said, 'I suppose we should. We asked the leasing agent to have it painted and the carpets cleaned. We really ought to see what condition it is in before we rent a truck and start moving.'

"Susan, her husband, and their children accompanied our family on the drive to our house. The outside had been painted and the lawn was wonderfully green. We unlocked the front door and flicked on the lights. We were transfixed. We were incapable of doing anything other than stand in the entry hall and stare in amazement. The furniture was arranged just as it had been all the years we had lived there. Books were on bookshelves. Further inspection revealed dishes in the cabinets and linens on the beds and in the bathrooms.

"'I would not have wanted to face moving and jet lag,' Susan sheepishly admitted. 'The only thing I couldn't remember is where you had hung each painting, so I just stacked them in the den.'

"'The least we can do is hang our own pictures!' I responded as I reached out to enfold her in a hug. 'You've done everything else!'

"Because of Susan, our first night back home was literally at home. We slept in our own beds, between our own sheets. Single-handed, Susan had organized and accomplished this great gift." Susan's eagerness to help stemmed from pure empathy. Susan just put herself in Sylvia's place and knew she would not want to unpack and move in those circumstances. Putting ourselves into our friends' place may not always be easy, but it is always an act of love.

A Sixth Sense

Our sensitivity to one another's health or state of mind often stems from undiluted listening and paying attention, our antennae dialed in at a very delicate setting. Occasionally we do not need to observe subtle signals to let us know a friend is in need. Beverly told us about how a friend uncannily knew when she was in trouble: "One day while we were at her house talking, she recalled that she was at a retreat once and all of a sudden my face came into her mind like 'bang'—she hit her hand to her forehead and she just started praying for me. She said that I must have been going through some tough stuff at the time. She was so right. It was amazing to me."

Janet, forty-three, also told us how her friend Chris just seems to know things about her in ways that do not make sense: "Chris and I have been friends since we were twelve. The night of my first child's baby shower I called her in California, where she had been living for ten years. I was on the phone telling her about all the gifts when the labor began around midnight. My labor turned out to be a long, slow one, so I called her a couple of times the next day to keep her posted on my progress.

"By 9: 30 that night I was finally off to the hospital even though the pains were still five minutes apart. I called her before I left so she could keep me in her prayers. It was 6: 30 P.M. her time.

"While I labored on through the midnight hour and all the early morning hours she was busy at work, running the restaurant she owned. She later told me she ended up with a tension headache after the usual, hectic Saturday evening crowd. She took a headache tablet, which she just uses on rare occasions because they always knock her out and make her sleep late the next day. After going to sleep around 1: 30 A.M., she woke up wide-eyed at 4: 15 A.M. and was unable to go back to sleep. This surprised her due to the usual effect of the medication. So she decided to call my hospital in Florida at 4: 30 her time to see if there was any news on me. The nurses told her I had finally delivered my daughter at 7: 14 A.M. my time (4: 14 her time). Whether it was my pain or joy or relief that transcended the several thousand miles between us, it was enough to wake her out of a deep sleep." Who can say that certain happenings are merely chance? Sometimes we stumble upon knowledge in circumstances that seem more than accidental. Perhaps this knowing is what some have referred to as psychic ability, spiritual wisdom, or the sixth sense.

Karyn told us this story: "Patty and I were both musicians and became friends in our high school band. Over the years we kept in contact and visited one another; she had remained living in the same city where she went to college, but I had moved all around.

"She was in my thoughts one sunny afternoon as I was puttering around in my kitchen. I was thinking that we had been friends for quite a while and wondered exactly how many years it had been. After doing the math, I realized that we had been friends for over fifteen years—and that she was my oldest friend.

"I was slightly amazed at how quickly the years had passed since we first met and how we stayed in each other's lives despite the fact that I was such a vagabond. I was struck with great affection, and I felt a deep commitment towards her and our friendship due to my new realization. I decided to sit down and write her a letter that very moment.

"Patty is not someone who is sentimental or who shows her emotions easily, so I didn't want the letter to be sappy or to make her uncomfortable. It simply read: 'I realized today that you and I have been friends for over fifteen years. I want you to know how lucky I feel to have you as my friend.'

"One month passed from the day I sent the letter, and there was a knock on my door. It was Patty and her partner, Ward, rushing into my house in a flurry. She yelled 'hello!' to my husband, who was still upstairs, and she and Ward ran around the house, playing with our Boston terriers and whipping them into a frenzy. After a while, Ward and my husband went out into the backyard with the dogs, and she and I sat down and started to catch up.

"She told me that things hadn't been going so well in her life for a while. She had been terribly busy with her career and had been working many hours and weekends. In the meantime, Ward had become interested in another woman and thought he might be falling in love. Possessing true respect for, and complete honesty with, one another, Ward kept her apprised of his situation so that there were no secrets and so that Patty had the power of having information to make her own decisions. She told me it was the hardest thing she had ever experienced and that she thought she might lose Ward forever.

"She then reached into her back pocket and pulled out a small envelope. The edges were tattered and worn so they were almost like fabric. Running her fingers over the frayed threads of the paper, she said, 'I got your letter. I've been carrying it with me every day.'

"They ended up working things out and I'm very glad because I truly believe they were meant to be together. I love Ward very much, and I understand that loneliness can sometimes cloud a person's vision. And, I am forever thankful that I reached out to my friend Patty through that letter — I had no idea what strength that little card was destined to carry.

"You know, I don't believe I possess any supernatural powers or a sixth sense or anything like that. But what I can tell you is that I do believe in the powers of love."

Whatever the source of this amazing connection, girlfriends for life are attuned to the other's feelings and thoughts. They can take the time to put aside their own problems to make the quiet space required for empathy and, if needed, action. And when we become a bit too cynical or analytical, mysterious timing and perfect moments remind us that some events and some relationships happen for a reason that transcends a merely logical explanation.

You Can Count on Me

Since the death of my husband at age forty-two, twenty-two
years ago, my sister-in-law has been a rock for me,
especially when I was diagnosed with breast cancer. She flew
cross country to take me out to buy a wonderful hat and
to a photography studio to have our pictures taken,
so that when I lost my hair, I could look at the photograph
and look forward to growing it all back.

—LOIS ALLARD

A girlfriend who values her friendships will make the effort to drag herself out of her own absorbing problems to hear about, and help with, her girlfriend's struggles. That is not to say that we are, or should be, selfless at all times, but that we cannot always be focused on ourselves if we are to be a true friend. Friendship is not all about one person being in crisis at all times. In a friendship for life, we help each other, being able to give as well as take. In fact, it is sometimes hard to know who is helping whom, as girlfriends take turns listening, talking to, and coming to the aid of, each other.

A Listening Ear

When hard times come, girlfriends listen. Candi wrote to us: "Breaking up with a boyfriend is never easy, especially when you think you've finally found Mr. Right. I was convinced this was the guy I had been waiting for and fell hook, line, and sinker. I really believed him when he said he loved me and wanted to get married.

"As if overnight, everything changed. I'm still not sure what happened. All I know is the man I fell in love with disappeared and in his place was this moody, uncommunicative guy who started backpedaling. I don't know what I would have done without my girlfriends during this time, who were supporting me and helping me face reality when I didn't want to. They realized it was over long before I could accept that, but they let me sort it out on my own time schedule.

"This guy, from what I hear, is going through the same pattern, supposedly falling madly in love and planning a wedding with someone else he's just met. I don't know if he'll come through for her or not, but I am certain that my girlfriends are with me for the long haul. Their love has helped me remember that I am lovable, even if this guy can't love me. I'll be forever grateful to them."

As Candi's story reveals, our relationships with

men can be a source of bliss . . . or not . . . and our girlfriends are often the ones we turn to during the *not*-so-blissful times. Janna told us that in college she "started dating a man I thought I would marry. I spent all of my time with him and very little time with Jennifer, my roommate. Eventually, this guy and I parted. It was the most painful time I had experienced to that point in my life.

"The night we broke up, Jennifer found me lying on my bed crying. She had a date, but when I told her my boyfriend had left me, she canceled her date and spent the evening with me. She did not think about how I had abandoned our friendship to spend all my time with my boyfriend. Instead, she came to my rescue and was a true friend.

"Knowing there were no words that could erase my pain, Jennifer laid down beside me and just let me cry and talk. She will never know how much that moment meant to me. She didn't hand me a tissue and go on her way. She made me feel comfortable by coming to my level and simply being there with me."

As Janna and Jennifer's situation illustrates, we sometimes show our support by simply being present with our friends. No advice is needed; no wisdom required. All we request is an understanding heart and a listening ear.

An Active Hand

In other situations, we may need the more active participation of our friends. Dana told us how her friend Heather "showed up" at a crucial time in Dana's life: "When I was a senior in high school, I got very sick and was required to go into the hospital every month for an overnight stay for chemotherapy treatments. It was strange, being in high school and being sick— everyone else is just carrying on their high school routine around you and no one really knows what to say to you about your sickness. It's awkward, and going into the hospital every month was lonely—my boyfriend would be out with his friends and I would be having this experience that none of my friends shared. Then one night as I was sitting in my hospital bed, my friend Heather just showed up, carrying in my favorite junk food, and she sat with me through the evening, watching a beauty pageant on television. Just having her come in as if she were walking into my bedroom at home made me feel so normal. I will never forget how much fun we had that night watching the pageant—in fact, it started a tradition between us. Now we are in our twenties, and we still get together to watch beauty pageants on television."

Jenni wrote in and told us about her good friend who stood by her when others who should have did not: "My friend is very special to me, and I owe her dearly for being around when I've needed it the most. I got pregnant at the age of twenty-one, and my boyfriend, the baby's father, decided he didn't want to be a part of my life or the baby's. I decided to place my son for adoption to two wonderful people.

"My family was very supportive, but if it hadn't been for my best friend, I would have had a tough time. She went shopping for maternity clothes with me. She would go out with me to eat or to the movies, when everybody else was out having a wilder time. She spent hours on end walking through malls and looking at Christmas lights with me when it was close to my due date, hoping that the exercise would help the baby come faster.

"The most wonderful thing she did was coach me through my labor. She withstood nine hours of screaming to witness my son being born. I couldn't have done it without her. She helped me pull through something that has changed my life forever—pregnancy, birth, and the adoption process. She still is supportive of me even through this past year when I've struggled with my post-partum depression and grieving process. She helped me through the most difficult time of my life. If that isn't true friendship, then I don't know what is."

Dena told us a similar story about how her girlfriend stood by her when it seemed like her life was coming apart. She had a period in her life when one difficulty after another presented itself: "My story begins in February 1993, when I found myself single and pregnant. Although my friends had strong opinions, most contrary to my own, they did not waver in their support of my decision to have my baby. Not only did they stand by my decision, but they planned the baby shower, were with me the night I went into labor, were there to welcome my daughter on her first day in the world, and have become the best aunties any little girl could ever dream of having.

"In June 1994, while vacationing three hours north of my hometown, my daughter suffered a severe seizure. She was placed on a respirator and spent three days in an intensive care unit. I placed a frantic and hysterical call to my friends, and before I knew it, they had driven over two hundred miles to be with me and my baby, staying with me until she recovered.

"Then on January 31, 1996, my father committed suicide. Needless to say it was shocking and traumatic, but thank God for my friends, they pulled me through again. From that first moment they were by my side, sleeping at my house those first two nights, then caring for my daughter for days and nights while I dealt with the reality of it all. Not only did they care for my little girl but they were at the wake, funeral, and my house, shining love and support throughout."

Even though her last few years have been difficult, Dena can recognize that "I have also been blessed because I got to see the strength and love of my girlfriends. I know that without their comfort and support I would not have come out of these past few years a sane person. I also know that with them in my life, I can face any catastrophe that may come my way."

Dena summed up the essence of friendship — they keep us sane, jump in when necessary and provide the silver lining to a dark cloud (or at least a messy one). When things are rough or we are going through transitions which turn our lives upside down, we can find a friend holding our hand.

Marlene told us this story of when a friend was there for her in a dark moment: "My best friend, Stephanie, and I had masterfully planned a weekend of hiking and fun with our dogs, she with our longtime friend, Stoli, me with my new puppy love, Cosmo.

"As I set out from Raleigh on I-40, it started to pour. Visibility was extremely low, and the highway was especially crowded despite my attempt to leave later to avoid heavy commuter traffic. I headed two hours down the road to Winston-Salem, windshield wipers frantically clapping. I was in the far left lane; the fast lane. Suddenly two vehicles immediately ahead of me locked up their brakes. My following distance didn't matter — the pavement was too slippery. I skidded into the back bumper of the car ahead of me with an amazing jolt. I started to tremble as I pulled my car over to the shoulder.

"I stepped out of the car, into the miserable rain, to assess the damages and to see if the other passengers were okay. There appeared to be no damage to either car and no personal injuries. After we exchanged phone numbers and insurance information, I went back to my car to resume my journey. No sooner did I open my door to get into the car than my frightened puppy bolted out onto the highway. I lunged to grab her leash, but she was too quick, and I was too late. I picked her bloody body up off the highway and carefully placed her in the back seat, hoping that she was still alive. My body was shaking. I sobbed uncontrollably as I raced to find a vet in the nearest town. It was too late; Cosmo was gone.

"I continued on my way to West Virginia, knowing I needed the comfort of my best friend more than ever. I cursed myself the whole way for not strapping her leash into the seat belt. She had always enjoyed riding in the car, knowing that she'd be going to some cool place. The jolt of the accident had startled her so that the last place she wanted to be was in that awful car.

"I checked myself into the hotel, burst into tears once alone in the room, and waited for Stephanie who had a much longer drive from Ann Arbor, Michigan.

When she arrived, I was a blubbering mess. I just couldn't shake myself of what had happened. I hugged Stoli for dear life, glad that one of our furry friends had survived the trip. Stephanie helped me calm down, then got down to the business of cleaning the blood from the back seat.

"I was awake crying all night, fading in and out of nightmares. Stephanie pampered me the entire weekend, reminding me of the things that had gone right and of what I had to offer the world. She wouldn't allow me to blame myself. I am forever grateful for her love and friendship and its power to soften tragedy."

Expanding the Circle of Love

When tragic things happen to the ones we love, they happen to us as well. Even though we may not be the person who is sick or in danger, we are nevertheless affected when those we love suffer, and we may find it difficult to fulfill other important roles we have. We need support from our girlfriends not only to relieve our own suffering, but so we can be there for those dependent on us. Marsha told us how important Tracy was for her and her son when Marsha's husband suffered a serious accident. She wrote, "Ever since our sophomore year in high school, Tracy and I have been close. I've considered her my very best friend ever since the day my husband was badly burned in an accident and required a six week stay in the burn unit at the University of Michigan Hospital.

"Without a second thought, Tracy was at my door with suitcase in hand. She moved in with me and helped me with my not-quite-one-year-old son. She got up with him in the middle of the night, fed him, and changed his dirty diapers, and best of all, she let me cry when I was scared and didn't know what had happened to my storybook life. I am happy to say it has been eighteen years since that awful day. That little baby is now in college, and I am still happily married."

Julie, now forty-four, told us how a friend she had not seen for years helped support her when she was feeling worried: "My mother, who lives in my home-town in the Midwest, had just suffered a heart attack and stroke. I came from California, where I have lived for years, to be with her, to help with any arrange-ments she needed to make, and just to monitor the situation. I called my good friend, Cheryl, whom I have been friends with since we were seven. We met at the lake where our families had summer cabins. She was now living a few hours from where my mother was hospitalized. We had talked on the phone several times during adulthood but I don't think we had actually seen each other for six or seven years. It was great to talk to her about my mom, whom she knows so well. When I hung up, I felt so much better.

"The next day, as I was sitting in my mom's hospital room, a woman appeared in the doorway. I kept looking at her, thinking 'it can't be her.' But there was Cheryl! She had decided after talking to me that my mom and I needed some support, so she got in her car the next day and drove to the hospital, several hours away. She took me to lunch and was just there for me. It gave me the strength I needed to get through a very difficult time. Every time I think about it, I get tears in my eyes. I don't know if she will ever know what it meant to me to see her dear, familiar face."

In times of crisis, a friend can make the difference between our being able to cope, or giving up in desperation. Brenda told us this story about Carol, a friend she'd had since the first day of high school in 1960: "In June of 1989, my husband was transferred to Tampa, Florida. It was hard moving away from Carol; I love her like a sister. Our friendship has had its ups and downs through the years, but we always managed to patch it up and continue on — that is, until December 1992, when I became annoyed at Carol for some reason (to this day, I couldn't tell you what it was). We didn't speak until June 4, 1993.

"I remember that date clearly because it was the day that tragedy came knocking at my door, knocking the hardest it ever would. My sixteen-year-old daughter, Danielle, was in a very serious automobile accident. She suffered a traumatic brain injury and was given a five percent chance to live. Nicole, my oldest daughter, knew that she had to call Carol and tell her what had happened, since I was not capable of making any phone calls.

"Carol called back, letting me know she was there for me. Throughout the three-and-a-half months Danielle was in a coma and for the next year, Carol called me every day, sometimes even twice a day, letting me know that she was there for me to talk to and to cry with. She gave me words of encouragement, sometimes calling just to say, 'Hello, I was thinking of you today, and I love you'."

Tragedy sometimes seems too much to bear. There are moments in our lives when we question whether we have the strength to go on. Tracy, Cheryl, and Carol gave their girlfriends the support they needed to carry on and do what was needed for their loved ones. Most of us suffer losses and disappointments that seem insurmountable, but when we do not have the strength within ourselves, our girlfriends can loan us their hope, their passion, and their commitment to life so that, on borrowed faith, we can take the next step.

Beyond the Call of Friendship

Many of the amazing stories of friendship we received showed courage, love, and valiant support, stories in which women described the actions of their girlfriends as "saving their lives." Most speak metaphorically, but sometimes girlfriends literally save the lives of their friends. One woman named Gayle wrote to us about the incredible courage and generosity of her friend Penny in a moment of crisis: "Penny and I have been friends for thirty years. I can still remember our first meeting and my first attraction to her as a person. She was everything I wanted to be — sophisticated, impeccably dressed, a college student, beautiful, warm, funny, and short! At five-foot eight, with a size twelve dress, a size nine foot, and a secretarial job, I formed an instant, but superficial admiration that has grown over the years into a genuine love and devotion for a one-in-a-million friend. Penny welcomes her friends right into her heart and lets you know that you are a valued and needed part of her life. Over the years we have shared joy and heartbreak on both sides — and much, much, laughter.

"I have had End Stage Renal Disease since my early twenties. I had two failed transplants, a hip repair, many surgeries, and eight-and-a-half years of dialysis by the time I was thirty-four. My husband and friends always pulled me through. In an experimental procedure I received my sister Michelle's kidney in 1984, even though we had incompatible blood types. My heroic sister had given me the gift of a new and wonderful life. After thirteen years of much happiness and good fortune, a wonderful career, travel, and shared good times with my husband and our wonderful friends, my kidney failed in June 1997. The next six months were the darkest period of my life. I thought I had lost everything: my job, my health, my world.

"When I had to confront the reality and go back on dialysis, I truly lost all interest in living. Penny was right there, feeling helpless and in pain alongside of me. Believing that there was nothing she could do to help me was torture for her. Little did she know. Many nights I would lie in bed and listen to her voice on my answering machine. 'Gayle, it's me. If you don't pick up the phone it's okay. I know how hard it is for you to talk, but if you need me, I'm here. I just want you to know I love you, and I'm here for you whenever you need me.'

"When we found out that the waiting list for organs was two years long, we knew I couldn't wait. I was having complications from dialysis nearly every week and deteriorating both physically and mentally. Then we were told by a physician that an organ donor does not have to be related to you—the organ can come from a friend. We told everyone we knew. My sister wrote letters. My husband wrote letters. We had eleven people volunteer to be tested! Among the first few, of course, was Penny. The rest of the story is about a girlfriend *extraordinaire*, about a lesson in courage and generosity, about the love of a friend that is indeed the love of a sister. Penny and I were an excellent match — in so many ways! She was in perfect health and had the support of her wonderful family and friends. On January 6, 1998, I received her kidney."

What an extraordinary gesture! The love that Penny showed her friend is unparalleled and certainly beyond the call of girlfriend duty. We hope that few ever have to ask for this level of generosity from their friends (and to be a good friend, we do not want to imply that it is a requirement to make the sacrifice that Penny made).

But since none of us know where the next turn of events will take us, looking to the future, with its uncertainties, can be a frightening prospect. However, our fears can be soothed by the certainty of friendship. Most of us know that, come what may, we can always count on the support, love, and active assistance of our lifelong girlfriends. We can all take comfort from our friends in many ways, and rest assured for now that we can rely on them for moral support no matter what comes our way.

We Can Make It After All

Tracy and I have been friends for twenty-seven years, and I think the secret to our friendship is our mutual respect for each other. Although our lives are so very different, we've always been so proud of each other's accomplishments.

—MARSHA KRAFT

Every healthy, loving relationship between two people requires that both individuals be able to tolerate the differences between them. Friends for life may share many things, but still have differing tastes in everything from what they eat to the life partners they choose. Respect for those choices and support of the differences can enrich the friendship and the friend's lives, as they witness, and participate in, each other's life paths.

Supporting Our Differences

A true friend recognizes and honors the individual she calls her girlfriend for life. That includes honoring that person's choices and beliefs, even if they are not shared by both women. Arlene sent us a letter about her unique friendship with Barbara, a friendship which thrives despite their different religious beliefs, or perhaps, because of them. She wrote, "'The soul of Jonathan was knit with the soul of David' (1 Sam. 18: 1). This Biblical paradigm for friendship became real for me on a hot night in July of 1964 when Barbara walked across the driveway that separated our two houses and extended a neighborly hand in friendship. The heavenly knitting needles went to work and haven't stopped to this day. My friendship with Barbara has continued since that first handshake, spanning more than three decades. And all but four years of that time we've lived two thousand miles apart.

"We have each crisscrossed the continent to attend each other's children's weddings. She and her family have traveled four times to Seattle for the bar mitzvahs of our sons. We have supported each other in times of joy, in times of sadness, in times of trials and tribulations, in times of illness, and in times of death. In 1997, she rejoiced with me when, at the age of fifty-eight, I was ordained as a rabbi, realizing a lifelong dream. The following year, along with her ministers, I laid hands on her when she was commissioned as a lay minister in her church. She knows the basic prayers of the Jewish worship service, and I joyfully join in the hymns in her Methodist church. I think it is our differences that bring us together. We seem to complement each other in many ways. When I describe my friendship with Barbara to others, I often say, 'She's an Indianan, rather conservative, Republican, and Methodist, and I'm not!'"

Allowing Change

Perhaps one of the most important qualities of a long-term friendship is the ability to allow room for growth and change. The bond between women can be challenged when changes that come with growing up and growing old confront a friendship. These changes come in all forms and create stress on the relationship, regardless of whether the new turn in the road is deemed as positive or as a tragedy. Events like graduations, job offers, weddings, and the birth of children are seen, at least on the surface, as experiences to be joyously anticipated and happily celebrated. Even the most exciting of changes, those for which we have toiled long in the classroom or carried for nine months in wondrous anticipation, place each individual woman in a different location in life in relation to one another. Graduation may mark the end of living together, weddings might leave one girlfriend single and the other with a new best friend, and the birth of children might result in one girlfriend consumed with new duties and responsibilities her childless friend can imagine but not fully share.

Jane wrote us about her fears and hopes for the future, now that she and her close friend Mandy have graduated from college. She said, "My relationship with my college roommate, Mandy, could be considered uncanny from the very start. The summer before we began college, we received information about our prospective roommate in the mail, including phone numbers. I don't remember who called whom first, but we hit it off from 'hello.' We had both been cheerleaders, National Honor Society members, your run-of-the-mill, all-American girls. We spoke several more times before we actually met. I so clearly remember the day I met Mandy. I was so excited to go away to college and live with this person with whom I had so much in common. I practically ran up the stairs to our dorm room and walked in to meet her and her parents who had just arrived. We embraced, the first of a million hugs to come, and immediately began making plans to decorate our room. It seemed like we'd known each other forever.

"That August it was over ninety degrees every day, and we used to sit in our TV-less room in our bras and shorts and play cards all afternoon. I dragged her out to parties and she dragged me to class. We were 'JaneandMandy'—one entity. For Halloween that year, we went to a thrift shop and bought two hideous dresses and cut them in half. I wore the top of one and the bottom of the other, and she wore the other two pieces. We went as Jan and Marsha Brady. We held hands all night trying to balance on the three-inch-heeled boots we'd bought.

"The next year we moved into a sorority house and were roommates again. During our junior year, we lived in separate rooms, but were directly across the hall from each other. Our senior year was a year of change. Mandy's boyfriend (whom I never liked) broke up with her, and she was crushed. I lent a shoulder to cry on while insulting this loser profusely. I knew she was so much better without him. Eventually, she realized this herself. Then she helped me end my relationship with my boyfriend, who wasn't good for me either. I am so grateful for her support.

"Over the four years in college, we ended up with the same major, even the same academic adviser. We were up until all hours of the night working on our senior theses. We'd yell back and forth across the hall (we could see each other from our desks). I'd continually ask her how to spell things, and she'd coax me into ordering pizza. She graduated with honors, and we both got accepted into different law schools. I was so proud of her, probably more proud than I was of myself.

"I remember that last day vividly. We were both moving our remaining belongings out of our rooms, still across the hall from each other. Suddenly I looked over at her and realized that we would never live this close to each other again. I felt sick. How could I live (or spell) without her? I quickly shoved the rest of my stuff in a bag, wiped away a tear, and acted like I was just going down for another trip to my car. But it was the last trip. I couldn't say 'goodbye' to her—partly because I would instantly begin weeping and partly because I knew it wasn't really goodbye. She called me a couple of weeks later and scolded me for just leaving, even though she knew why I did.

"This fall I'm moving to Pittsburgh for law school, and she's moving to Chicago. I'm heartbroken that I won't be able to yell across the hall to her, but I know if I need to talk, she'll always be there."

Dana told us this story about when she and her friend Heather were both going through big life changes simultaneously. "I moved to northern California a few years ago from Texas, where my best friend, Heather, was still residing. After living here for a couple of years, I met my boyfriend, Jeff, and after being with each other for a while, he and I decided to move in together. Right around that time, I got a call from Heather and she told me that she had decided to move to northern California and suggested that we live together. Jeff and I talked about it and we decided we would all share a place.

"It took about a month of living together to find out that this was not going to work *at all*. Although Heather and I had been inseparable when we were living in Texas, we had never lived together. All of our differences became apparent. She was a night person, I was a morning person. Jeff and I are both low-key personalities, Heather is very high energy and more emotional. Perhaps we could have survived all of that, but we were both going through such big changes that were very different from one another. She was just moving to a new city where she knew no one but me, and was relying on me to help introduce her to her new location, and I was becoming more intensely involved with my boyfriend. After another month of tension, we agreed that we would split up — Heather would find her own place and Jeff and I would move out to a smaller apartment. We were both angry and upset, and when the day came that Heather was going to move out, no one said a word to each other all day.

"When it was time to return the rental van at the

end of the day, Jeff wisely suggested that I go with Heather in the van, and he would follow in the car. We were sitting there in silence, and I was thinking of how much history and 'firsts' I had shared with this woman. Our friendship was irreplaceable. Besides, she was a great person! I thought our friendship was over, and I felt very sad. I guess she was feeling some of those same feelings, because all of a sudden, she blurted out, 'I'm sorry!' and I immediately responded, 'I'm sorry!' That was about eighteen months ago, and now Heather and I are as close as ever. Our friendship was rocky for a while, but I am happy to say that it is still intact. She is now good friends with Jeff, too, and is dating one of Jeff's coworkers. I think we are both greatly relieved that we survived that rocky period."

Although anxiety producing, Dana and Heather have made room for the other to be in different phases of life—and discovered there is still room for the friendship. Often friends who are adjusting to change see their shared experiences coming to an end, although, sometimes those changes can bring us even closer. Heather has found a new friend in Dana's boyfriend, and even a new boyfriend herself. After the initial, albeit traumatic, adjustment, the friendship has settled into a new equilibrium. Hopefully these young women will continue to redefine their relationship so that their bond will last a lifetime.

Starting Families

Graduation, career choices, and geographical moves are not the only events that can stress a friendship. As girls grow into women, many choose to include marriage in their life's path. Since it is rare that two close girlfriends marry on the same day, one woman enters a completely new life phase while the other stays in the single world. The joyous occasion of getting married can be tempered by a sense of sadness, even fear, at what impact this momentous change may have on a treasured friendship.

Because many times the basis for our girlfriend relationships arise from our shared experience, a change in one woman's experience can be frightening. Wendy told us about the resistance she has gotten from her girlfriend Paulette since she got married: "She makes me feel that I am selling out. She thinks I am too domestic, that I am no longer developing as an individual, or that I am too concerned with being in a relationship instead of being me. She seems very judgmental about what I do, but then she has also told me that she admires my commitment to my husband."

Paulette's problem with Wendy's choices may reflect Paulette's own conflicting feelings about the compromises necessary in a romantic relationship. On the other hand, her concern may correctly reflect the fact that Wendy is not taking care of herself. Probably the truth is somewhere in the middle. Everybody's life situation changes, and unfortunately, no two women change in exactly the same ways at exactly the same time. The good news is, if each woman is allowed the space to change, these differences can be enhancing, and growth can deepen a bond between them.

Problems arise, however, for those who do not make room for their girlfriend's partners, often forcing their girlfriends to choose between them and their romantic loves. When an ultimatum is given, the romantic partner is usually chosen and the girlfriend is left behind. A story we heard from Ginger captured this heartache: "I didn't like Terri's boyfriend from the start and was glad when they broke up. About a year later, they started dating again. Looking back, I can see why Terri didn't tell me she was dating him again, since I had been so verbal in my dislike of him. She and I were talking on the phone one night about a party I was hosting, and she asked if she could bring him. I groaned, 'Oh, no. I don't want him at my party.' There was silence on the phone, and then she said in a soft voice, 'Ginger, he and I are engaged.'

"Boy, had I stuck my foot in my mouth. I tried to backpedal but to no avail. Even though she included me in her wedding plans and actually asked me to be a bridesmaid, a bond had been broken between us.

She never felt safe to talk about him with me, and to be honest, nothing I could say would change the fact that I really did not like him. I wanted to, but I didn't.

"Not surprisingly, after they married, Terri and I lost touch. They moved about two hours away, and I didn't see her for several years. But like many good friends, we eventually made contact again, first through some business dealings and then personally. With a few years of mellowing and the experience of dating a couple of men my other girlfriends didn't like, I had a new perspective on passing judgment on other people's choices. I genuinely apologized for my behavior, and she forgave me. We made peace and are still good friends.

"Perhaps the best part of this story is the way her husband has reached out to me. Recently my father passed away and, during a work day, both Terri and her husband came to the memorial service. I was moved by the effort it took to attend. Oddly enough, my father died the day before my birthday, so there were no celebrations that year. Her husband hugged me and said, 'I was saying to Terri that week, isn't it close to Ginger's birthday? We should send her a card.' I was stunned that he even knew when my birthday was, let alone remember it and mention it to Terri. I realized that there was much more to this man than I'd ever given him credit for, and I regretted the years of separation my judgmental attitude had cost us all. It's taken time, but finally I see there is room for all of us in Terri's life."

Allison wrote us about a transition she faced: "Last June, Amy got married; therefore, I got divorced. Let me try to explain. Amy is my identical twin sister and my best friend. We've been a pair for as long as I can remember. But her marriage to Mike defined a new pair of which I was not a part. This was difficult for me to accept for a while, because I saw her wedding as the symbol of losing a part of myself and certainly losing my best friend. So, I essentially saw their marriage as our divorce. Our relationship would never be the same . . . or would it?

"Recently we spent the entire day together, just the two of us. It was like old times. We thoroughly enjoyed ourselves. The next day, Mike, Amy's husband, made a comment that shook me a little and made me reflect on my relationship with her. He turned to my sister and said, in a teasing manner but with a sensitive undertone, 'You have more fun with Allie than you do with me!' After much denial and attempted reassurance to Mike, Amy stopped a moment, listened to her heart and replied, 'You know what? You're right. Sometimes I do.'

"I hadn't realized how difficult it must be for Mike to be married to a twin and to feel at times like he can't compete with the closeness we share. Now I understand that it has probably been just as hard for him as it is for me. I also realize just how powerful Amy's and my friendship is and how important girlfriends really are in one's life. Friendships may shift and alter, they may strengthen and weaken, but the bond of a true girlfriend can never, ever be broken."

The birth of a child was also the topic of several of the stories we received about change and adaptation. Conflicts, questions, and concerns can be raised when one friend has a child and the other one does not. It is the friends who are committed to the friendship, and who are flexible to accept these changes in their friends' lives, who keep their connection through the birth of a child. Rose, now pregnant with her first child, talked to us about how her relationship may change with her friend Diane, whose child is nearly grown and out of the house: "One thing that tends to happen is that when you have kids, you tend to develop relationships with other people who have kids. Then your old friends are still single, or maybe they are married and don't have kids. You drift when things are a little different. You have to consciously say to yourself, 'Okay, I've got to work more on this relationship.' I think about Diane and how I am just starting out when her only son is probably going to be out of the house in a few years. This is going to take some work, but I can't

99

envision my future without her."

As these many friends discovered, marriage and babies do not need to mark the end of a friendship, even though it may indeed signify the end of an era in that relationship. Recognizing that no one can take your place in your girlfriend's life is a necessary aspect of maintaining a relationship that can span a lifetime. If friends can make room for each other when they are making changes in their lives, they can set the groundwork for sharing a great number of life experiences that will come their way, each at different times and with varying impact.

Changing Roles

As the friendship between identical twins Amy and Allison illustrates, lifelong friends come in all sizes and shapes and can even start out as relatives. Sisters have become best of friends, as well as mothers and their daughters. A parent and child may especially have difficulty with this transition, however, if one or both of them only sees the other in the particular role of "mother" and "daughter," without seeing the other as a person and potential friend. Sally told us about how she and her daughter, Stacy, turned a significant corner from relating as mother and child to relating as adult friends. She said, "My husband and I were married about four years before I became pregnant. When I became pregnant, all my girlfriends knew that I wanted a girl first. I looked forward to having someone to have tea parties with, to go shopping with to buy that favorite little girl dress, and ultimately, to having someone with whom to plan a wedding. In September of 1972, we were blessed with Stacy, a darling little girl.

"During the years that Stacy was growing up, I don't think that our relationship was any different from any other mother and daughter. We had our times of conflict — times when we disagreed, times when she was grounded and the car was taken away from her, and times she would 'talk back' or want to stay out late. Like most teenagers, there were times she didn't want me around. We didn't always see eye to eye. But that is what love is about, to allow others to disagree with you while, at the same time, realizing that the relationship continues on. I always tried to be there for her.

"My husband and I decided we wanted to make our house a place where Stacy and her friends would want to spend time. So we built a room that had a black-and-white checkered dance floor with strobe lights, a mirrored ball, and an old juke box. It was wonderful because all the kids came to our house to hang out.

"When Stacy went out, I usually waited up for her until she came in at curfew time. She always knew that I would have something ready to eat for her and her guests. We would stay up for a while, and she and her friends would sit and laugh and talk and tell me stories about what they did that night. Most of the time all they did was cruise town and spend time with their boyfriends, but they always knew that I would listen to their stories. I have a lot of fun memories.

"When she decided to go to Indiana University, her dad and I were thrilled because that was our *alma mater*. When she told me she wanted to join a sorority, I was hoping she would choose the one I had been in. When the choices got down to two, one of the ones that was left happened to be mine. She told me that when she visited the sorority, they were singing my pledge class song, the same song that my pledge class had written twenty-three years previously.

"She called me in tears once she got back to the dorm, and said, 'Mother, for your sake I wish my first choice was your sorority, but there is another one that I think I would be happier in.' I was so proud of Stacy because she was making a decision for herself, not for me. I drove to the university the next day and surprised her by being there when she got her bid from the other sorority. We went out and celebrated. Stacy did what was right for her and not what was right for her mother. I believe girls have to be strong enough not to do what their moms want all the time.

"A few years later, when she fell in love and began to plan a wedding, Stacy moved back home before she got married. She and her fiancé had decided to have a really large wedding—with bridesmaids and a sit-down dinner—a Cinderella day. She came in one day and said, 'Mother, I have decided who I want in the wedding and who my matron of honor is going to be.' I said 'That's great. Who are the girls?' So she named off the bridesmaids, and then she looked at me and said, 'I would like you to be my matron of honor.' Well, the chills came and then the tears rolled down my face. I look back at that time, and I realize that that was the defining moment where I became not only her mother, but her best friend. It really was exciting.

"We spent the next year having a ball doing all the girl things you do with weddings. I think about how I got to walk down the aisle right before our daughter did. I stood up at the altar next to her and held her flowers while she and her husband said their vows. I had his ring on my little pinkie. It was one of the proudest moments of my life.

"It's easy to think about all of the little petty times you may have with your daughter, but if you stick in there, you definitely get the gratitude that mothers deserve. And a good girlfriend as well."

When we asked Sally what she thinks inspired her daughter's loyalty and friendship, she said, "I think that you must treat each other with respect. I think that is the main thing." As a mother who is also good friends with her daughter, Sally knows what makes a friendship work. She raised her daughter to make her own decisions, and she respected and honored those decisions. This goes for any friendship. What we found in our interviews and the letters we received is that if we cannot respect the decisions our friends are making, if we cannot adapt to the changes they choose to make, the friendship will ultimately not last.

New Friends

A serious relationship, a marriage, or a child can threaten the status quo in a friend relationship, but we found that if another girlfriend appears on the horizon, it can also trigger fears of rejection. We heard from Grace, who wrote us about a problem she's had. "It seems that my friend Kimberly, whom I grew up with, is jealous of Judith, whom I met a couple of years ago. When the three of us are together, Kimberly is always so negative it brings us down. I've mentioned this to Kimberly, but we haven't sorted it out yet. I don't want to chose between these two friends, but it appears that I'm moving closer to Judith and further away from Kimberly. It's hard for me because I've shared so much with Kimberly."

New people come into our lives throughout our lives, and if we become possessive of a particular girlfriend, demanding that she choose between us and others, we run the risk of losing her. There is a delicate balance between guarding the friendship and allowing it to change as we change, while protecting the precious uniqueness of a lifelong relationship.

What is right for one person may not be right for another, or at least not right for right now. We have to remember not to take our friend's choices personally — she is probably not getting married, moving to take a new job, or having a baby because she is trying to avoid us! If a friend's life changes, we should graciously respect and adjust to this change. It is important to keep her in our life, even if she is more occupied with other things at the moment. And if we are the ones doing the changing, a simple declaration of devotion to our friend ("My life is taking a different turn, but I need you more than ever because of it!") can go a long way toward assuaging her fear that you might be dropping out of her life forever.

Commitment

Is any friendship easy? Most of the time —yes; other times, no way! Coming together to create a special bond requires a commitment to that relationship. Friends for life are trustworthy and loyal, standing up for each other when needed, and challenging each other if necessary. Creating a relationship that lasts, at times, requires that girlfriends speak up when something is wrong between them, confident that the truth will not sever the bond.

What is the glue that holds a friendship together? As these stories demonstrate, commitment to each other is the foundation to longevity; a commitment which includes the gumption to face conflict and wrestle to resolution.

We Can Tell Each Other Anything

We all live on bases of shifting sand, [and] need trust.

—ERMA J. FISK

A friendship worth keeping forever could never be maintained without trust. Girlfriends learn over time that we can trust each other with the things most precious to us. As we experience the other as trustworthy, we start to share the thoughts and fears we otherwise would guard most zealously. We heard one woman say about her friend, "I trust her with my home, my money, and my boyfriend. Most importantly, however, I trust her with my secrets." One aspect of trustworthiness is the ability to keep the many secrets we share over tea, discuss during breaks at work, and whisper to each other before the movie starts.

Keeping Secrets

Any relationship between women in which one person feels that she has to hold back part of herself is one which is limited in its potential. Ellen illustrated that the inability of a friend to keep a secret places limits on their friendship: "I have a friend, Alice, who just cannot keep her mouth shut. She doesn't mean to be malicious, but she accidentally tells things she should not. So, there are certain things I cannot share with her.

"For example, at one point Alice, another friend named Janet, and I were all working together at the same place and Janet was getting involved with a man who was friends with some of our coworkers. She wanted privacy and therefore did not want the relationship talked about at work. We made sure Alice didn't know the details of that relationship as long as she was working with us, because we were aware that if she knew about it, then everyone else we worked with would know too.

"Alice's untrustworthiness definitely inhibits the relationship. I really like her, but there are just some things that Janet and I do not divulge to her because we don't want other people to know. Janet and I will actually get together, maybe an hour before the three of us are scheduled to meet, and decide what we feel safe sharing with Alice. A couple of times when we have all been together, Janet and I have made eye contact and have shaken our heads 'no' when one of us has started to say something. Alice is a wonderful person, it is just that we know her too well and we don't want to put ourselves in positions that could end the friendship."

It seems to us that Alice is fortunate to have such understanding girlfriends who will maintain contact with her even though she has demonstrated that she cannot keep confidences. After all, if you can't trust your girlfriend with your secrets, who can you trust?

Perhaps the clearest example of betrayal we've seen in recent days is the broken trust between Linda Tripp and Monica Lewinsky. When the news came out of Linda Tripp's taping of her "confidential" conversations with Monica Lewinsky, you could hear the gasps of women all over the world and a collective: "She did what?!" Imagine your best friend sharing all your secrets with everyone. While we certainly do not condone Ms. Lewinsky's behavior, we have gleaned from women everywhere that the first rule in any girlfriends' code of ethics (the unwritten rules of friendship which all women somehow know and most adhere to) would prohibit Ms. Tripp's behavior. Regardless of one's politics, one thing that true girlfriends agree upon is that keeping secrets is an essential requirement of friendship.

While disclosing a confidence is a betrayal, so is the use of that information against someone. One woman, Marta, told us about how someone she thought was a friend constantly moved in on any guy in whom she showed an interest: "I had a friend in college I learned could not be trusted when it came to anything involving men. In fact, she was outright competitive with me. Whenever I told her I was interested in a guy, she would immediately go after him. I learned not to disclose my interests in men because she would always pursue them and even go behind my back and make phone calls to them. It was bad and ultimately destroyed our friendship."

When trust is missing, friendships stand little chance of deepening, and may instead fade away in the future. However, we are not suggesting a one-strike-and-you-are-out rule. Most people have done things that were not trustworthy, especially in youth, when we are learning what is acceptable in friendship and what is not. In addition, sometimes genuine mistakes are made; we may not know information is confidential or we may erroneously assume another friend already has the information. A good guideline is to assume nothing. If the information would make us uncomfortable if it were revealed about *us*, then don't reveal it about anyone else. And never use information to serve your own ends! But if a mistake is made, apologize and learn from it. If the experience of betraying a good friend does not stop with once, followed by a sincere apology, it is a good bet that that relationship, like Marta's, will be short-lived.

Because confidentiality is a fundamental component of women's friendships, the girlfriend bond has, in many cases, taken on near sacred status as a safe place to confess misdeeds, admit failures, explore remedies, and, purely and simply, tell the truth. A friend for life feels privileged to hear our innermost secrets and our private fears about ourselves; concomitantly, girlfriends for life treat confidences as they are treated in confessionals and the therapist's office. Talking honestly about ourselves, mistakes and all, and trusting that our girlfriends will not betray us, are significant components of the girlfriend relationship.

Learning to Trust

Most women expect trustworthiness in their girlfriends before true closeness can be achieved, but other women have to learn that vulnerability, *their* vulnerability, is required in order for them to achieve closeness with other women. For deep friendship, we have to be able and willing to trust another person. Rita told us how it took her years to fully trust her girlfriend, Briana, not because Briana was untrustworthy, but because Rita was fearful to let anyone know her true self. She said, "When I was in my twenties, I lived a double life. I had my good-girl persona, which I showed to most of the people I knew, and then I'd date men who weren't good for me; relationships I knew would not receive the approval of my friends and family. For several years, I kept these two parts of my life separate. Even my closest friends didn't know about the different men I was involved with.

"Then I got into therapy and began to realize the role my low self-esteem played in my choices in men. Perhaps even more profound was my discovery of the way I hid the truth from myself and, therefore, from others in my life. I decided to trust one person, Briana, with my whole story. I'd known her for years, and she had been the best of friends to me. The parts of myself I did entrust to her had been carefully protected and nurtured, so I knew she was up to the task. But was I?

"I got together with her and told her I had chosen her as someone I wanted to be fully honest with. Her eyes got a little wide when I told her about the men I'd dated and the trouble I'd gotten into, but I could sense that she never pulled away from me emotionally. In fact, when I was finished with my tale, she told me she was honored that I had trusted her with this information, and I could sense that she was being genuine.

"Even though Briana never demanded that I change in any way, somehow being honest about how I allowed men to treat me caused a transformation in me. Accepting her love through trusting her made me want more for myself. Soon after that conversation, I broke off with the relationships that weren't good for me and started dating men I was willing to acknowledge and invite to meet my friends. I now see that I felt alone, not because there weren't people in my life that I could trust, but because I wasn't taking the risk of letting anyone else really know me."

Sometimes our ability (or inability) to trust can be challenged by unusual circumstances. Beverly told us this story of how her friendship with Felicia sprang from an unexpected encounter at the beach, an encounter that forced her to address her hesitancy to trust: "It was two years ago in the summer. I was at the beach with my two sons, sitting on my blanket, doing nothing, and this woman walked over to me and asked me if I was by myself. I told her I was. I forgot her exact words, but she explained her situation to me.

"It turned out that her ex-boyfriend's cousin set her up to bump into her ex-boyfriend on this day at the beach. She felt awkward because she didn't want to see him anymore. So in order to avoid talking to her ex she made up a story and said that she spotted a friend on the beach and was going to go talk to her

117

(that's when she saw me). I felt so taken by her honesty, and I decided to play along with her. We pretended to be old friends that day. Then, as it turned out, she didn't live too far away from me, and I ended up giving her a ride home.

"I had just been betrayed by several people in my life whom I considered very important to me, so I was very cautious about trusting anyone new. But I was moved when she trusted me, and our relationship developed from there.

"Today I consider her a dear friend and she feels the same about me. She says that she feels God brought us together. I still admire her because she is not afraid to show her true feelings." Many times in friendship, it seems that we are destined to rescue each other. Felicia and Beverly came along at the right moment for each other, with Beverly helping Felicia, and then Felicia inspiring trust in Beverly, who had not been able to trust for a long time.

A friendship for life requires that each woman be trustworthy, and that they also have the ability to trust. But if we have difficulty trusting, our girlfriends may give us the faith to trust again or even for the first time. Vicky talked to us about how her close girlfriends have slowly helped her move from a place of self-imposed isolation, to a place of openness and trust: "I started out in life not trusting anyone, whether they were male or female. My family situation was very difficult. When I did venture out with my mother or father I could see it was dangerous and unwelcome. No one in my family spoke honestly to each other, not even me and my sister. She and I had grown up in the same difficulties and with the same secrets, and never dared to talk when the two of us were alone. I became unable to talk to anyone about anything important.

"I remember only having 'at-arms-length' friends during my school years. To make matters worse, we were always moving. I went to four elementary schools, nine schools in all by the time I graduated from high school. I didn't know how to trust, and I never had the chance to learn. As soon as I'd begin to attach, I knew we'd move again. That tearing apart leaves an ache; a sound I can hear in my mind.

"As I got older, in my teens, I would try small toe-in-the-water relationships, but I didn't reveal much because it felt too risky. Then I had the experience of falling in love and having sex for the first time, thinking that we were getting married. I thought once we made love, we'd be able to talk to each other with a depth of intimacy I had dreamed about. But it didn't happen. He wasn't a bad guy, he was just a teenage boy having sex for the first time, and verbal intimacy wasn't something he understood at that point in his life.

"I was devastated by this disappointment, wanting

my emotional isolation to end with my experience of physical intimacy. Out of the pain, I turned to a girlfriend who was more sexually experienced than me. I asked her, 'Oh my god, what's going on with my body?' I needed to talk about what I'd felt. She was wonderful in her understanding, her acceptance. We talked about so many personal things. This opened the door for me, a firm foothold into the rich relationships that are possible with other women.

"This was my first girlfriend, but not my last. Over the years I've known women who've proven to be impeccable human beings. Each one has taught me that trust is possible. Sonya, the woman who has most recently come into my inner circle, took one of my classes. I teach poetry as a therapeutic or spiritual practice. At the end of a session last year, Sonya asked me to teach her to do what I do. Over the years, I've had about forty people ask me and I've never said yes. But it was easy to agree to mentor Sonya. I felt that she was the student I'd been waiting for all my life. I knew she already had the gift within her. All I have to do is point to it, and all she needs is some remembering.

"I owe a debt of gratitude to all the other women friends I've ever had who taught me so much about trusting other women. By the time I met Sonya I had so much trust in myself that I was able to fling myself into this relationship and trust her immediately. As a poet, I go into my creativity—what I refer to as the darkness from which all things come—a wonderful abyss. I have always gone alone. But now, for the first time, I have the chance to go there with someone else, someone who shares my passion for language."

What a gift—a friend to whom we can confess our fears and with whom we can share our deepest misgivings and intimate thoughts about ourselves. An invaluable and loving cycle starts when we begin to trust other women. As they prove themselves trustworthy, we begin to trust our own instincts even more, and can quickly ascertain whether new people we meet are worthy of our true selves. Through learning to trust her friends, Vicky is seeing the good that is possible from other relationships. Starting by trusting a friend, she can begin to consider the possibility that she need not always be alone.

No Shame Allowed

Trustworthiness is about having faith that someone will keep your secrets, will react in a loving way to whatever you reveal, and accept you without making you feel ashamed. Eleanor told us about her friend of fifteen years, Jasmine: "One of the attributes of my friendship with Jasmine that I so appreciate is how I can tell her anything. Not only do I know that whatever secret I tell her is going to be kept confidential, but I can tell her things about myself or my actions that I am embarrassed to tell anyone else. She never makes me feel bad about myself, no matter what I tell her. It is not like she pooh-poohs my problems either. She always listens, and she will tell me what she honestly thinks without making me feel ashamed."

Knowing that we can say what we really think and feel without rejection provides us with a safe haven in which we can say the unthinkable, the feelings we are not "supposed" to entertain, and allows us to cleanse our hearts. Dot and Diana, girlfriends through thick and thin, have shared many happy times. They have also shared pain and anxious moments, such as when Diana's baby boy became quite ill. Diana wrote, "Dot and I have been friends for eighteen and a half years. We each had daughters, and three years after their births, we shared the desire to have a second child, which we both hoped would be boys to round out our families. My son, Matthew, was born on January 26, 1982. Unfortunately, he was born very ill with a congenital heart defect that required two open-heart surgeries and resulted in numerous complications. It was the worst year of my life.

"My husband and I struggled with the fear of losing our precious little boy. There were so many times that year when Dot knew exactly what was needed. The day I came home from the hospital without my son, she met me at my house with a table cloth, cloth napkins, and turnovers. While our daughters played, we sat over coffee, and I felt complete. I could talk or not talk, either was accepted. Even though she was eight months pregnant, she took the hour-and-a-half trip to Boston's Children's Hospital to visit me as I sat by Matthew's intensive care crib after one of his surgeries.

"The day that sealed our friendship for life came when Matthew was about four months old. He was not doing well at the time. I remember having a house full of people. Dot and I snuck out with a bottle of wine and went down to the local beach. We sat on the beach and drank the wine, and she allowed me to verbally plan his funeral. It sounds very morbid today to say this, but at the time it was something I needed to face. Everyone else insisted that I have positive thoughts and wouldn't allow me to share my fears. Thank God we never had to have the service I planned that afternoon, as my son has survived these many years, but having Dot there to listen, without judging, and to accept me and what I was feeling meant more to me than anything else.

"I have learned a lot from Dot. We have never judged each other's decisions, rather we've listened, offered advice, and then sat back to rejoice in each other's successes or mourn each other's losses."

Diana was able to relieve herself of a great burden that day, the thought that the worst could happen and her son could die. She needed to be able to acknowledge that possibility without being chastised or made to feel guilty. Dot gave her a trustworthy place to spill her thoughts—a place without shame, a place without guilt, a place of love.

Girlfriends for life are trustworthy women who are able and willing to provide a sanctuary for each other, listening as the other talks regardless of how acceptable their underlying feelings might seem. Where others might pass on bits of information as gossip, our true girlfriends value our confidences, protecting our private truths as they would their own, and accept what we have to say without judgment. If you find a woman who can be trusted, and who is willing to trust—keep her (along with the secrets she will entrust to you), and together you will build a bond that can withstand the test of time.

We Stand Up for Each Other

My girlfriend's ex-boyfriend refused to return her blender, and she was in no shape to see him again. I called and left message after message on his machine, but he refused to respond. Finally, I left a message saying, "I'm coming to your office tomorrow to make a scene." The blender mysteriously showed up on my girlfriend's porch that night. Sometimes we need someone to put our foot down and set things right.

— PAMELA SCHRAEDER

Our lives would be extremely difficult if we had to fight all our battles alone. Knowing that someone is "on our side," feeling we have the reinforcing support that we need, can prevent our being overwhelmed when trouble comes. Loyalty can take many forms. Sometimes it consists of just *not* being disloyal. Holly talked about how she was grateful for the way her friend Susan stood up for her when Holly was not around to know the difference. Holly said, "Susan knew my boyfriend Simon first, and actually introduced us. After Simon and I broke up, she stayed friends with both of us. She hasn't taken sides and has balanced things really well, being there for both of us as a neutral party. In the first couple of months after we broke up, Simon was being really negative about me, criticizing who I was and what I had done. She told me she said to him, 'Look, I know that you guys have had problems, and I know that it is hard, but I'm not going to sit here and listen to you badmouth her like that.' She stood up for me without necessarily taking my side. I admire that."

Helping Us Stand Up for Ourselves

Loyalty can also take the form of urging us to ask for what we want or need. Our girlfriends may show loyalty by rooting us on as we stand up for ourselves. Rose told us, "I have a friend who is always watching over me. A few years ago when I was considering a new job, she made a list: 'I've thought about it, and you need to make sure that you get this and this and this.' She will always ask, 'Now have you considered this?' making sure I've thought through all the angles. She is a little tougher than me, the one who has got the edge. I always think that is kind of funny, her own way of mothering me. She seems to think that I am some sort of sheltered flower that needs to be protected."

Standing Up to Us

A loyal friend may also step in when we are hurting ourselves. Sometimes our friends stand up *for* us by standing up *to* us. If they see us making choices or taking action which they feel will eventually hurt us, they try to stop us from following a self-damaging pattern which we cannot discern ourselves.

Of course, girlfriends have been known to be opinionated, so we walk a fine line between forcing our own judgments on our friends, on the one hand, and, on the other, reminding her to do what is best for her. Alison told us that her friend Elizabeth was concerned about her when Alison's husband was ill and admitted to the hospital. Alison said that when she called Elizabeth to tell her about it, Elizabeth focused on what Alison needed to get through the ordeal. "One of the first questions she asked me was, 'Are you taking care of yourself?' And I thought, 'Well, no, of course not!' I was taking care of my husband, and her insistence made me angry. But then, her comment stayed in my head, and I would occasionally think to myself 'Okay, I do need to walk outside of this hospital.' So her comment gave me permission to step back from the situation a little. But she was so didactic about it that it annoyed me. When other people asked me the same question, they seemed to present it in a different way, and I experienced it differently."

The act of reminding someone to take care of themselves can come across as preachy, or it can be helpful and loving. In this case, as in many others, it seems to depend on the delivery. Although Elizabeth was really trying to be loyal and protect her friend from overextending herself, Alison heard disapproval in Elizabeth's tone and felt defensive. The secret is to take our sense of approval or disapproval out of the equation and deliver our concerns in a caring manner, which will be more effective in the long run. If we remind a friend to take care of herself in a judgmental way, she will probably resist us. If we say our concern, or even pose it as a question, in a way that gives her room to think about what we are saying without feeling she needs to protect herself from our judgment, she is more likely to see our point and make the change.

Natasha will never forget how two of her closest friends provided a model of self-care in a devastating situation: "My husband and I had been married for twenty-nine years and were in real trouble. We decided to separate, and I found myself in the most painful period of my life. Two of my friends were incredibly supportive to me, although in very different ways. One friend, Jenny, was so loyal in her efforts to just be with me and let me express whatever I was feeling. I especially remember a time with her when I was feeling devastated, it seemed that my heart was literally breaking, and I laid my head in her lap and wept. She just let me do that, sitting with me, not judging me, not being angry at my husband, just giving me the permission to feel whatever I felt. That moment is so vivid—I remember where we were, how our bodies were situated, how my sobbing sounded. It was an intense, deep experience for me.

"My other friend, Rita, was also so loyal to me. I went to see her for a few days, and after a few hours of talking about some of the details of our lives, she built a fire and we started talking about the real stuff. The tears started to flow. We began the first of many long, intense talks about my life. Rita confronted me with so much that visit: I needed to nurture and love myself; I needed to find my center, my soul; I needed to push outside my comfort zone; I needed to let go of the control I've exerted over myself; I needed to go away on a spiritual retreat. She advised specific actions, detailed ways in which I could take care of myself. I felt more and more scared and confused, and wondered why I had come to see her. But I knew the answer. I knew myself that I needed to do these things, and I needed to figure out why I had been so frightened about this change in my life. Our time together pushed me closer to knowing what I must do.

"What both of these friends did for me was to

provide a model for me to take care of myself — Jenny taught me to help myself heal by letting all the anguish come out, and Rita guided me on taking steps to face the next phase of my life. What neither of them did was get judgmental on me or attack my husband. They didn't want me to poison my marital relationship with anger, which left me the option of reconstructing my relationship with my husband. Rita even pointed out that living apart from my husband didn't necessarily mean the end of the marriage. And she was right. All this happened about nine years ago, and after being apart from my husband for a year, we got back together again. Now our relationship is much better than it ever was, partly because my friends taught me how to be loyal to myself, how to focus my energies on taking care of me instead being angry with my husband."

Natasha's friends were loyal to her by encouraging her to express herself and do some soul searching in a time of marital crisis. Similarly, one of the authors of this book, Tamara, will always be grateful to her friends for sticking by her and encouraging her toward a new career: "I was a corporate lawyer for six years, and I did not like my career, but I kept trying to pretend to myself and to others that I did. I had too much invested to just give it up, and I was convinced that if I kept at it, I would eventually feel differently.

My friend, Laura, and I worked together at the law firm, and she was unfailing in her support of me. When I was upset or angry or frustrated over my inability to get out of my job and try something new, she was there to listen to me and suggest some possible solutions. If I was in a real state, she would say something like, 'Where is the tammycam? I want to record this so I can play it for you when you tell me that you think you will start liking your job.' She would always make me laugh, and although I was annoyed by my own reluctance to make a change, she never treated me with disdain. She was much kinder to me than I was!

"Many of my friends provided that support and encouragement. Finally, I made the decision to leave the law and to go into publishing, a career I had never considered until it was suggested by another close friend, Betsy, who knew how much I loved books. My dear friend Linda wrote me a recommendation for a publishing program that I was considering entering. My girlfriends were incredibly loyal to the person I was and the person they knew I wanted to be. They supported my decision, assured me that I was not crazy for jumping into an entirely new career, and helped me figure out problems which came up in my new business. I am much happier in my current career. Without their listening, their genuine concern, and their thoughtful and sometimes humorous (but nonjudgmental) prodding, I don't think that I would have had the courage to do what I did."

Standing Up on Our Behalf

Loyalty includes instances of friends cheering us from the sidelines as we try to make positive changes in our lives. But there are times when we know we can count on our friends to draw from their fierce "mother bear" energy and stand up on our behalf. Sometimes we need an advocate when we have not been able to address a problem or when we are overwhelmed in a situation. We have stories of women who, in a variety of instances, took matters into their own hands on behalf of their beloved girlfriends.

One woman still feels grateful to her friend, Maureen, who helped with an annoying problem: "My friend has really been good about encouraging me to get what I want. If I buy an article of clothing that I don't like when I get home, she will say 'take it back' because she knows that I am the type of person who will not bother with it. Sometimes she just steps in and takes control. There was a time when I had just returned home from a European vacation. In the midst of the fog of my jet lag, someone called me on the phone and sold me, for thirty-five dollars, one of those coupon books for discounts at community businesses. They assured me I could return it if I didn't like it.

"When I received it, I could see that the coupons were nearly unusable by me — they were all for things like having your nails done between two and four P.M. on Tuesdays on the other side of town from where I worked. I decided I was going to return this book. Well, I didn't send it certified mail, so I had no proof that I sent it back, and pretty soon I started receiving letters from this company saying I owed them the money. I said that I had sent the coupon book back, and they denied it. Then I started getting letters from a collection agency!

"I complained about this several times and was just going to send them the money so my credit would not be ruined when my friend Maureen, who is a lawyer, decided she had heard enough. She said 'I'm writing a letter.' I've always told her that she writes the best nasty letters of anyone I have ever known. She sent this letter off for me, and I actually received a letter of apology from this collection agency! She stood up for me, and I'm very glad she did!"

A common scenario in which women stand up for each other is in time of sickness. When we are ill, we may not think clearly about how to best take care of ourselves. Additionally, when weakened by an illness, an otherwise capable woman can be rendered helpless to effectively advocate for herself. Tracey wrote us about a time in college when she stood up for her girlfriend Anna Maria and got her the medical attention she so desperately needed. First, she needed to stand up to Anna Maria, to make sure she got help. Tracey told us, "Even though we shared the same living area, Anna Maria and I didn't bond until she got the flu. She was terrified of doctors and refused to go for medical help. Eventually she grew too weak to argue, so, with the help of another roommate, we physically carried her to the car. I took her to a nearby 'doc-in-a-box' where the nurse helped me carry her inside.

"Anna Maria was sick and scared and wanted me to stay with her in the exam room, even though the doctor insisted that I leave. At only seventeen years old I don't know where I got the nerve, but I told him that he would treat her with me there or we'd go find another doctor. He didn't like it, especially when she got hysterical at one part of the exam and I made him stop. He made it very clear that he wished I was on another planet!

"I stood my ground, or, more precisely, I stood her ground for her because she was unable to do it for herself. When he recommended that she be hospitalized for dehydration, she refused. Somehow I had the presence of mind to ask what could be done to avoid it. He said that she had to consume a quart of fluid an hour, every hour, for three days. I agreed to be responsible for making her do it. I guess he figured I was stubborn enough to succeed, so he sent us home. She got well, and we have mother-henned each other through countless adventures and misadventures since then."

Standing Up for Those We Love

In some instances, we need our friends to advocate for us, while other times we need them to step in on behalf of those we love. Bobbi will be forever grateful to her dear friend Debra for taking charge when Bobbi's father was seriously injured in a car accident. Bobbi, her mother, and Debra stood in the emergency room, overwhelmed at the sight of Bobbi's dad strapped to a back board, face cut and bleeding, with his neck and legs broken from the accident. Looking around the emergency room, Debra realized that this was their worst nightmare come true—nurses were scarce, the doctor was nowhere to be seen, and Bobbi's father was delirious and trying to pull his neck out of its brace. If he had succeeded, he could have become totally paralyzed.

Moving into action, Debra instructed Bobbi and

her mother to go home for clothes so that her mother could spend the night at the hospital. Once Debra had them out of the room, she held down Bobbi's father's arms to keep him from further injuring himself. Bending close to his ear, she said softly, "Our Father, who art in heaven" and then stood up and shouted to the nurses in the next room, who were huddled around a computer screen, "Get the #*%& over here and help me!"

Two nurses scurried over and helplessly said, "The doctor didn't give us orders to restrain him." Furious at their lack of concern, Debra loudly demanded that they call the doctor immediately to update the orders. She then turned back to Bobbi's dad and softly said, "He maketh me to lie down by still waters." Looking up, she saw the nurses hesitating to make the call, and she yelled loudly, "I will make sure you &%#* regret crossing me. If anything happens to this man under your care, I'll have your @$#*# on my mantel! I want him cared for and up to the ICU in the next *#@* thirty minutes or else!" Dropping her voice again, she said kindly, "Thy rod and thy staff, they comfort me." She flipped back and forth from quoting scripture to cursing like a sailor to get the situation under control. When Bobbi and her mother returned, her father was calmer, restrained, and being moved to the intensive care unit.

Stepping into Our Shoes

One of the most significant ways that we can stand up for each other is for a friend to literally take our place in our absence. Jane told us about two women who were so close that when one of them died, the other stepped in and raised her three small children: "Marilyn and her friend Myrtle Rose grew up together and had always said that if something ever happened to one of them, the other would be there for them. Neither expected that time to really come, until Myrtle Rose became seriously ill and it became apparent that she would not recover.

"Marilyn was married to Charlie, and at the time of Myrtle Rose's illness, they had two grown daughters, about twenty-four and twenty-one, the last one having just graduated from college. They had come to the time of their life when the kids were out of the house and they could relax a little bit. Myrtle Rose had married later than Marilyn, and after Myrtle Rose and her husband had three children, Myrtle Rose's husband died. One of the complicating factors was that Myrtle Rose's husband had been German and they lived in Germany. In fact Marilyn was visiting her there when it became evident she was to live only a few months longer.

"Marilyn returned home, and she and her husband

agreed that they would serve as legal guardians of the children, one boy, who at the time was eight, and two girls, aged eleven and thirteen. At the time, the little boy had no memory of being around a man because his father had died early in his life. Marilyn and her husband flew to Germany so Charlie could meet the children, and they could start the legal and financial processes in motion for taking these children from where they were born, their home, to another country.

"They flew to Germany and in the last few days before they arrived there, Myrtle Rose became critically ill. She died just shortly after they arrived. Rather than have several months to do all the things they had to do, they had about a week to make all the arrangements to move the children to the United States, to decide what they wanted to do with the furniture, clothes, and keepsakes, and what to take and what to leave behind. And, of course, attend the funeral and face the loss of Myrtle Rose. It was very traumatic.

"But when you are in a situation, you just do it. And that's what Marilyn and Charlie did. Once they brought the children to the States, it took about six months to get them all in school and into the activities they liked to do. There were so many details to work out, like their immunization records. All three of the children had records, but they were in German. When they took these documents to the pediatrician to put the information into the computer, they had to find someone at the office who could decipher German. Fortunately, Myrtle Rose had made the immigration arrangements earlier, so they had no trouble bringing the children into the country.

"At first it was overwhelming for all of them, especially Marilyn. She had worked most of the time when her own children were home, at least after they went to high school. Now she was again inundated with washing dirty clothes, cooking regular meals every day, getting the kids to ball practice and music lessons, and things like that. She left her job so she could really be there for these kids. I understand that the young boy who had never been around an adult male very much has really become involved with her husband and they have formed a really close bond. They are all making a positive adjustment.

"I admire Marilyn and Charlie for being more than people who talk about friendship. Myrtle Rose's children couldn't be in better hands. I'm sure that Marilyn and Charlie prayed about it a lot and believe they had spiritual guidance to do it. It comes down to the fact that Marilyn and Myrtle Rose were really close, closer than real sisters. Even though they had lived apart so many years, they had kept up with each other. What may start out as perhaps a simple conversation over tea, 'If something happened to me, would you take care of my children?' can become a life-changing promise. It takes someone like Marilyn, the kind of person who is very compassionate and takes her word seriously, to actually step in and follow through."

Women's friendships have, in the past, been overlooked or trivialized in movies, television shows (remember Alexis Carrington?), popular fiction, and the media (there is nothing that sells like a cat fight), relegating us to a class of petty individuals whose only concerns are competing with one another, gossiping, and shopping. As we can see, however, the bond between women can be profoundly compassionate and protective, surviving longer than the lives of the women themselves. Friends worth keeping stand up for us, stand up to us, and stand in for us in situations when we genuinely need to rely on their love. In those times, they are our Rock of Gibraltar, to whom we can turn for the strength we need.

We Need to Talk

A friend is someone who is there for you in the good times and the bad, and will be honest and truthful even if it hurts. They don't just tell you what you want to hear, they tell you the truth.

—MARSHA KRAFT

We have found that women can talk about anything in the world to each other and yet be reticent to speak up when it is time to share a negative feeling about the other. Perhaps the hardest thing for women to do in a relationship is to be honest about their feelings, especially if it might hurt or upset their girlfriends. When we have spoken to women about relationships that have not weathered the test of time, we have often heard comments like, "I knew something was wrong and that she was upset about something, but when I asked her, she just said, 'Oh, nothing.' And then we gradually lost touch with each other." Oddly enough, many women may let a friend drift away rather than risk experiencing conflict. Lifelong friendships, much like successful marriages, require being honest, dealing with disagreements, and working through hurt to the point of forgiveness.

Speaking Up

Many women have never learned to express their irritation or hurt feelings to one another. One sure way to lose a friend is to pretend you are not hurt when you actually are, or to try to hide your anger. Conversely, as the next story from Lynette illustrates, once our feelings are shared, we can take the relationship much deeper: "My girlfriend, Josie, and I had been friends for several years. We originally met at work and found we really enjoyed each other's company and sense of humor.

"After knowing each other for quite a while, and frequently spending our free time together, we decided to go on a trip to Europe for two weeks. Well, we just about strangled each other. We had both been under a lot of stress trying to get away on this trip, and by the time we were on the plane, we were exhausted and short on patience. Additionally, the difficulty of traveling in a foreign place can add its own anxiety. Every peculiarity of our personalities came out. I found out that when Josie is stressed, she has no appetite, and she found out that when I am stressed, I eat like I will never have another opportunity. So there was a constant tension around food—she wouldn't think any restaurant looked appealing, so we would go trudging from place to place, looking for something acceptable. I would be starving. Josie later said that when we would finally eat, I would sit like a vulture over her food, fork poised while asking, 'Are you going to eat that?'

"In retrospect, we find these memories hysterical. But at the time it was tough, as we had never been in a situation where we were irritated with each other. Plus, both of us were 'good girls' who never felt free to express a negative feeling to someone we cared about. Finally, months after the vacation was over, one of us made some wry comment about the trip to the other and the floodgates opened. We were able to start talking about the interactions between us in a calm way, and we laughed at our eccentricities.

"The thing is, our friendship is much better now. We understand what makes each of us tense and why, and now we are sensitive to each other's peccadilloes. The other day she and I were talking, and I was really cranky and a bit snappish. When I heard myself being bitchy, I apologized. Josie said to me, 'I think it is great that we can be cranky with each other. We know it is not going to end the friendship.' And she was right. It is a great relief to both of us."

The Courage to Fight

Once Josie and Lynette realized that irritation or out-right conflict was not going to destroy their friendship, they could start dealing with conflict when it came up, instead of waiting for months. It takes faith in the friendship to speak up as soon as something feels wrong. Vicky told us how she has grown confident that she can argue with her friend Martha and know it would not destroy their relationship: "Martha and I have been friends for thirteen years and have many things that bond us. For example, she's the godmother of my children, we share a love for learning, and we respect each other's work. I always felt behind her in some way, and it wasn't until five years or so ago that I was able to talk about that. From then on, I've felt like we were equals; we've both 'arrived' in our individual professions. The love of our lives is our work.

"But what really altered our relationship and put us on even footing was the test of having a fight. Not only did we get into a serious disagreement, we did it in public! Martha and I were teaching a class together called Women, Passion, and Devotion. She does a lot of body work and breath work, visualization, traditional therapy. I teach poetry writing techniques and creativity.

"She was presenting to the class and started talking

about studying in India. She said that for her, Sanskrit was a more 'prayerful' language than English. I contradicted her in front of the group and said, 'I'm sorry, but I can't have you saying that. English is also prayer.'

"She said again that for her, the sound of Sanskrit was more spiritual than English, and once again I told her I had to contradict her. I said, 'I'm sorry, I can't let you remove English as a way to pray when this is the very thing I want to teach them in writing poetry.'

"Martha held her ground and said, 'I don't think you're hearing me.'

"I said, 'No, I don't think you're hearing you. We're about to write prayer, in English, not Sanskrit, and you are accidentally stealing this opportunity from the class.' No matter how we approached it, we couldn't resolve the matter. Everyone in the class was white. I turned to the class and said, 'This is okay. It's the kind of conflict you can have with people that you love and work it out.' So we broke for lunch.

"We went off to lunch and continued our discussion until finally she saw that her comment took the possibility of writing poetry as prayer out of their minds as long as they were using English. She came back to the class and apologized, saying, 'I know you were scared, but Vicky loves me enough to stand up and say this to me.' We've talked about it several times since then. It bonded us even more deeply. She told me she felt honored by me. In fact, as she has thought about it, she realized that she'd also stolen English as a prayerful language from herself. Now she is writing in English more, deepening her spiritual walk."

Being able to get angry with one another indicates that women feel secure in a friendship, safe enough to show negative feelings. Joyce explained that she is now in the middle of the conflict process with her friend Melissa: "My mother was recently very sick and in the hospital. I heard from Melissa only once during that time. I felt that she did not step up and support me at all, and that was really hard for me. I was trying to figure out how to talk to her about how I felt, but I hadn't gotten there yet.

"Then she called one day and asked if I wanted to get together. I said okay—I knew that would be a good opportunity to sit down and talk about it. But every time I get angry at her she knows about it before I tell her; she can really sense my feelings. So she called back about five minutes later and said, 'What is going on?' We ended up having a long discussion in which I told her how I was disappointed and upset with her.

"We are still working on things, talking back and forth. She has said, 'I'm sorry. I screwed up. I feel like I wasn't there for you.' But there is always a 'but.' One of the things that she gets upset with me about is that she feels that I don't share with her enough about how

I feel. That has been an ongoing issue in our friend-ship, and she brought that up in this situation. I felt that I was in crisis, and I needed her to be calling me, but it's true that I didn't let her know exactly what I needed. I felt abandoned because she didn't initiate towards me, and she felt that I needed to be more clear about what I needed from her. It's clear that we both have areas to work on in this relationship."

The fact that these two women could tell each other about their dissatisfaction and their feelings is a good sign for the longevity of their friendship. Friends who are upset with each other and do not tell one another tend to drift apart—their discomfort prevents them from contact.

The discussion process, although perhaps painful and uncomfortable, also provides us with another ben-efit. Talking honestly with a friend can unravel not only mysteries about the other person but also about our-selves. Sometimes the greatest gift a friend can give us is the insistence that we do some introspection and un-derstand why we are upset. In Melissa and Joyce's case, the discussion will perhaps help Joyce learn why it is difficult for her to ask for help, and Melissa may understand why she was reluctant to rush in and be by Joyce's side during that stressful time. As we struggle to make our friends understand how we feel, we may uncover some surprising knowledge about ourselves.

Recognizing Our Limits

Perhaps one of the most painful moments in a friendship is when one girlfriend realizes that her friend needs or wants more than she can give. One woman told us, "A good friend of mine was grieving the death of her sister, and she genuinely needed a lot of support. The problem was that I had only so much to give at that point in my life. I felt horrible knowing that she wanted me to call every day, and yet I'd barely enough strength to face my own problems. I knew she felt like I wasn't there for her.

"We were talking on the phone around that time, and I decided to say what I felt out loud, even though I was shaking a bit. I said, 'I know you need more support than you are getting from me. I feel bad, but this is all I have for you right now.' She paused, and I know it hit her a bit hard, and she replied, 'Yes, I've been there for you in the past, and I feel like you aren't coming through for me.' I agreed with her but couldn't make the situation any different. I said, 'I am your friend, and I love you, but your grief is bigger than I can bear by myself. I want to keep you in my life but I encourage you to reach out more to other people as well.'

"That was a hard discussion. The next few days were a bit tense between us, but my friend is a strong and courageous woman. She realized that I had my limits, but that what I had to give was valuable to her. So, she joined a support group to get more help. She's met another woman in the group who is grieving the loss of a family member, and they're becoming good friends. It smarts a little knowing that she is bonding with someone else, but it is also a relief to feel like I'm not her only lifeline."

Like this story illustrates, we all have our limitations, which can disappoint both ourselves and our girlfriends. It takes courage to talk about these disappointments and negotiate a way for both women to have their needs met. But a friendship that becomes lopsided can be a relationship winding down. Both women need to be able to ask for what they need, and place limits on what they give. This delicate balance is rarely, if ever, maintained perfectly, so hurt feelings, misunderstandings, and forgiveness are required for the bond to endure.

Learning to Forgive

Working through a rough period in a friendship requires us to be empathetic with one another, placing ourselves into the shoes of the other and sometimes apologizing. If our friend has done something to forgive, we have to be willing to do that as well. One young woman, Ricki, wrote to tell us about her gratitude for her circle of friends and their ability to learn from, and forgive, each other: "I moved to a new school in fifth grade, where I didn't know anyone. There was something about this girl sitting next to me that caught my attention. Right then I knew she and I would become close friends, and I was right. Before the end of the first day, Claire and I had talked, giggled, and exchanged telephone numbers. We became best friends.

"Then seventh grade we met up with two other girls, Gina and Janelle. Four was so much better than two. Things seemed to be going great until one day so many things happened. Claire got mad at Janelle for something very small. Instead of staying out of it, Gina and I went along with Claire. We kicked Janelle out of our group. Looking back all fourteen years of my life, I will definitely say that was the biggest mistake I had ever made. We thought everything would be fine with Janelle gone, but we were wrong.

"In the meantime, Gina had problems that neither I nor Claire could help her with. All the while Claire and I were struggling with Gina, Janelle was in hell. We gave her dirty looks in the hall, teased her, spread rumors about her, and much more. Then out of the blue comes the worst thing that happened to me in my eighth grade year—Claire was moving.

"I refused to believe it at first, but when it came

down to those last few weeks I would be able to spend with her, I sat down and said 'Okay, this is it. It's really going to happen.' Our last day together, I spent the whole day with her, crying my eyes out and trying not to think of my life without her. In the last note she wrote me before she left, she said, 'I truly believe that your friends make you who you are, and I wouldn't be who I am today if it weren't for all those yesterdays with you.' Every day, I wake up and remember those words, and I know that when I look in the mirror I will be seeing a part of her. She and her mom drove me home that day, and we sat in her car crying for a while.

"Then I realized that sometimes you have to let go, even to the person who means the most to you, so I got out of the car, walked into my house, and didn't look back until I got inside. I saw her car driving away down the road; my eyes still water whenever I think about that. The next thing I had to worry about was what to do at school the next day. Her locker was right next to mine, and she was in a few of my classes. I cried myself to sleep that night, and even though I looked horrible, I went to school the next day because I had to be there for Gina. Together we made it through, not tear-free, but we made it.

"There was still something missing besides Claire — we needed Janelle. Janelle was the strong one in our group, and we always ran to her for comfort and un-

151

derstanding. Janelle needed us, too, but would it ever be possible after what we did? About a month and a half later I started a simple conversation with her. I could tell she was afraid of becoming close to me again, but could I blame her? Soon we were able to talk about the whole fight and eventually forgive each other.

"Right now we are all friends and just as close as ever. We still keep in touch with Claire, who lives in Florida, and we see her whenever we get a chance. The fight eventually brought us all closer together as friends. I am so grateful that Janelle forgave me, because if she hadn't, who knows where I would be?"

In Ricki's story, we can all recognize the drama, the painful machinations, and the tender, exposed feelings of adolescence. But before we dismiss Ricki's experience as childhood growing pains, we can see in her account the bravery of facing up to one's mistakes, the importance of forgiveness, and the value of our friends. Ricki is lucky to have learned these lessons so young. No matter how old we are, we can see ourselves in her story. Who, at any age, doesn't find themselves getting annoyed by something we realize is essentially petty? Who doesn't deal with difficult feelings in a relationship? The sooner we learn from our mistakes with our friends, and develop the ability to apologize and the capacity to forgive, the longer our friendships last.

Tracey told us about the forgiveness she and her friend, Rachel, have offered to each other in the years after they unwillingly met in sixth-grade health class: "We were all lined up against the back wall of the classroom as the teacher gave us the dreaded seat assignments. We had never met before that day, but, as we found out later, we were both praying not to be seated next to 'that girl' (each other). Of course, we were. We managed to ignore each other for the entire quarter. God being more stubborn than we were, we ended up in the same homeroom the next year. For whatever reason, we chose to sit next to each other, and before the first week was over, we were inseparable. We stayed that way even after I moved to another school our sophomore year.

"During our junior year, we had an argument that split us up for more than a year. By the end of our senior year, I had decided that our differences weren't enough to keep me from seeing her graduate. I found her after the ceremony, expecting to be told I had no right to be there. Instead, we took one look and fell into each other's arms. We picked right up where we left off. The events that parted us were forgiven and forgotten. I couldn't tell you what that fight was about if my life depended on it.

"Years later, we had a split again. This time it was my fault. Rachel moved to Michigan with her husband shortly afterward. She wrote me a couple of months later, and I wasn't mature enough to let things heal. I still regret that. A year later, on her wedding anniversary, it hit me like a bolt of lightning: I had been a bridesmaid in her wedding. If I let the relationship go, she would look at her own wedding pictures with regret. Whether she would regret having me in her wedding or regret losing the friendship, I didn't know. I was overwhelmingly sad when I thought of her daughter (unborn at the time) asking 'who that lady was' and being told 'It's just someone I used to know.' That thought broke my heart.

"So, I poured that broken heart into a letter begging forgiveness. I told her that if she didn't want to resume the friendship, I understood. I just didn't want her to look at her wedding pictures with pain. I hoped that my apology would give her peace. Well, being the generous soul that she is, she welcomed me back with open arms. It was like going home after a long, wayward journey. It has been over five years now. She has since given birth to that daughter I was so worried about and then a son last year. I have gotten married and have begun the process of having my own family. We have proven that our love will weather the hardest storms and years of separation. Her friendship, in the face of all that has happened between us, is one of the most precious things in my life."

Once we learn to speak up and fight with each other, we can start "putting our weight" on the friendship, confident that it can withstand some pressure. But when we speak the truth, we have to be able to listen and empathize with each other, say we're sorry, and forgive when necessary. Forgiveness is one of the most important qualities in keeping a friendship vital for the rest of our lives. No one does everything perfectly, and we will make mistakes with people close to us, even our best girlfriends—and can that make us feel terrible! As Tracey and Rachel's story illustrates, however, it is never too late to try and clear the air with a friend we have wronged. Apologies and forgiveness combine to make the magic that gets us beyond those mistakes and helps us set our relationships right.

Courage

Girlfriends for life help each other find the courage to get through everything from rough days to life-changing decisions. Our shared laughter and fun puts matters into perspective, even in the bleakest moments, and we encourage each other to take the steps in life that are right for us. We may first learn from our friends that we are valuable human beings, worthy of pursuing our dreams. Our self-esteem is shored up by their love and attention. Through our girlfriends, we are emboldened with humor and confidence, and when we need that extra nudge to go in the right direction, we can count on them to get behind us and push.

We Have More Fun than Anyone We Know

She always knows exactly what I need to boost my spirits and is forever doing the things that bring huge smiles to my face.

—AIMEE OLIVO

Often the words "fun" and "laughter" are mentioned when women describe their woman friends. Girlfriends worth keeping forever enrich our lives with humor and mischief, regardless of how "old" we become. We seem to revert back to giggles and allow ourselves unladylike guffaws over matters that only those in the friendship circle seem to appreciate. More than one woman has told us how she and her girlfriends find themselves to be absolutely hilarious in each other's presence, while everyone else who happens to be around them in those situations just rolls their eyes or stares in disbelief.

Just Between Us

Allison admitted that she and Amy, her best friend and also her identical twin, share a sense of humor others just do not understand. She wrote, "Recently, I realized how strong and unique our bond and friendship is. We spent a day skiing in New Hampshire—just the two of us. We had the most incredible day. It's so hard to describe the pure fun we had. All we did was laugh. Anything can be funny to us, things that no one else understands. We would say a word or a phrase and leave the other in hysterics for the next half hour. Our entire day was one laugh after another—so much so, it began to hurt!"

Shared laughter and inside jokes can begin when girlfriends are still girls and continue long into adulthood (when we are supposed to know better and behave ourselves). Debbie wrote us about her girlfriend and "the one remaining vestige of our teen years together, a language we share called 'Alfalfa' talk. It's a double-speak that a mutual friend taught us, and we are probably the only two adults on the entire planet who still speak this way when we don't want others to know what we're saying. I'm sure we're a sight, two grown women speaking in a 'foreign' tongue, even though it is English."

Perhaps our inside jokes are so rewarding to us

because they make us feel like we belong somewhere — that even if no one else gets it, there is at least one other person who understands why something is so darned funny. It is one of the least expensive private clubs there is — one which we can revisit in our minds for the rest of our lives. We may go to great lengths to recreate those times of fun. In the process, we create new memories. Shelley told us about how she and her three close friends Sue, Lynn, and Kathy keep finding new ways to get together and celebrate their connection. She wrote, "Sue, Lynn, Kathy, and I have been friends for over twenty-five years. The four of us became close during our college years; we were practically inseparable. Kathy, Lynn, and I commuted to a local college, while Sue worked full time. Kathy's boyfriend at the time (now her husband of sixteen years) dubbed us 'The Squad,' and from that point on, that's how we were known. Many years later, I had gold charms made that said, 'The Squad.' They hang on chains around our necks whenever we get together."

And celebrate, these four women do, with a flair for the fun and dramatic, even though they no longer live in the same towns. For example, three of these friends put their heads together to plan a surprise fortieth birthday party that would never be forgotten. Shelley described, "As Kathy, Sue, and I discussed how Lynn would be forty in February, crazy, wonderful plans started to formulate. The next day, Kathy contacted Lynn's husband, Steve, and I called my travel agent. Steve was so thrilled about our plans to come out and surprise Lynn, he told us he would send the four of us to a lovely local resort for two nights as part of his gift to Lynn. It was our first visit to Michigan (Kathy and I live in different towns in Connecticut, and Sue now lives in Virginia) and the excitement was building as we imagined the look on Lynn's face when she saw us. Steve met us at the airport, and we laughed as we hugged him.

"'She has no clue,' he said as we headed toward their home. Boy, was he right! The three of us burst through her kitchen door throwing streamers, screaming 'Surprise!' and 'Happy fortieth!' as a stunned Lynn stared at us in disbelief. Then there were tears (many, *many* tears) and hugs. It was beautiful, and we were quite proud of ourselves.

"The two days spent in Michigan were probably the most memorable we've ever experienced together. We ate, drank, played Balderdash™, and laughed till we cried. It snowed everyday as we shopped, worked out at the gym, gambled, told new stories, laughed about old ones, sang, screamed on the elevator ride, and toasted ourselves and our husbands.

"Our last night together, we said, 'We can't stop now!' With Kathy's fortieth birthday in September and

Sue's in November, we once again made crazy, wonderful plans. We flew to Kathy and her husband's condo in North Myrtle Beach for five days over Columbus Day weekend. The Squad was together again; Squad necklaces adorning our necks. The weather was perfect as we sunbathed, body surfed, walked and ran along the beach daily, ate, drank, played Balderdash™, and laughed . . . always laughed. Many gifts were exchanged during those five days, one of them a gift from Lynn . . . a book titled *girlfriends*. We have decided to continue our mini-vacations (big birthdays or not) at least once a year to celebrate our most treasured gift to each other — friendship."

Healing Fun

Laughter and fun keep friends coming back for more. Our shared humor not only makes us feel part of a select group where nothing has to be explained, but also provides a safe place to heal in times of trouble. Who has not had a rough day at work or a fight with a mate, and upon calling a girlfriend, ended up laughing at the end of the conversation? Vanessa told us this story of humor bringing relief: "Earlier this semester, my girlfriend, Cecily, and I were both having a very hard time. The weather was unusually dark and unrelenting, the mood on campus was depressing, and finals were upon us. I had been in my house writing papers, not sleeping or eating, for four days. Periodically I'd cry, I was so worn out. I didn't know it at the time, but Cecily was doing the same thing.

"After finals were over, I called her and said, 'I don't think I've left the house since last week. Want to go to dinner?' So we went out to dinner together, pouring out our woes to each other. Then something set us off, something minor, and we started giggling, then laughing so hard it was embarrassing. Weeks of stress and depression were shaken out of our bodies as we cried with laughter. When we finally got a grip on ourselves, Cecily said, 'I haven't laughed that hard for weeks.' It was true for me too. We cried out of relief. All we could manage to say was, 'More napkins please!'"

Our friends can help us put things into perspective and point out the humor of our situation. And when times are really grim, our friends' humor may save us from despair, even when the laughter might arise out of what seems to be a tragedy at the time. Sometimes when even a smile seems inappropriate, shared laughter with a friend can relieve mind-bending distress.

Judy recalled such a time, not long after she and her brother's fiancée, Laurie, had grieved the deaths of both Judy's mother and Judy's brother, Laurie's husband-to-be. She wrote, "Despite the somber thread that binds us together, whenever I think of our relationship, I think of laughter. We bring out the childish, playful, and sometimes sinister, side of one another. We share what we call 'the wicked laugh,' the one that we use when we're ragging on someone else.

"Months after my mom's and brother's death, Laurie and I took a trip to New York. We visited my mother's two sisters who lived in separate units within the same senior citizen complex. One night, we found the doors locked and the lights out at my Auntie Margaret's place. We knocked on the door to no avail. Finally I peered in the window to see Margaret laid out on the floor.

"A familiar pang stabbed at our hearts. Having lost my mother and brother in such a short period of time, we assumed that we were in for yet another 'character building experience.' Always the pragmatists, we began talking about how we could handle all the funeral arrangements—after all, who knew better about that than us? But then we realized, first things first.

"'Go get Aunt Nellie!' I shouted at Laurie. I can still see her long figure racing into the night on three-inch spiked heels, her raincoat flapping in the wind as she went for help.

"I peered through the window one more time at the corpse of my beloved aunt. Then it dawned on me that Aunt Margaret was from my mother's side of the family—hardy Irish folks who loved a good drink.

"'Aunt Margaret!' I called out.

"'Yes?' she answered without budging.

"'Are you okay?'

"'I'm fine!' she responded as though she were merely sitting in her chair, knitting an afghan.

"When Laurie, and my now frantic Aunt Nellie, came rushing up to the house, I met them halfway to give them the 'all clear.' Laurie and I attempted to lift Aunt Margaret from the floor and onto the chair. 'Bend, Aunt Margaret! Bend!' I commanded as my aunt, stiff in her stupor, refused to fall into a sitting position. I knew better than to catch Laurie's eyes, for the hysterical laughter was just beneath the surface and seemed to be escaping like steam through our pores. All we would have needed was one short look at one another to set us in motion. With a few taps at the backs of her knees, Aunt Margaret finally relented and allowed us to prop her up in the chair.

"'I don't know how that happened,' Aunt Margaret said over and over in her thick Irish brogue. 'It's not like I was drinkin' or anythin'.' On the contrary— in the excitement over our visit, and due to the fact that I looked so much like her recently departed sister, Aunt Margaret had downed the bottle of Johnny Walker we had brought her as a gift.

"With our lips sore from biting down on them, we politely excused ourselves to go to bed. Fortunately, we were sleeping at Aunt Nellie's house, which was far enough out of Aunt Margaret's earshot to allow us the time, distance, and freedom to explode on our walk there. I'm certain we woke the whole neighborhood as we howled through the complex.

"Throughout the years, Laurie and I have found ourselves in similar situations, literally crawling to the bathroom to keep from 'losing drops' as we call it, laughing over some outrageous thing we've said or done. We've been accused of being drunk or crazy—often both—but we're merely laughing the kind of laughter that sends your head back, makes your jaws ache, and causes tears to run down your cheeks."

Judy described her healing laughter with Laurie as letting the steam out. Often the fun that we enjoy with our girlfriends stems from letting the bad girls within out for a time. What is it about our friends' presences that inspires us to make mischief, take revenge, and strut our stuff? We think it is the strength we derive from our friends, not just in times of trouble, but when we are at play and enjoying ourselves. We not only laugh more, but we tend to laugh a little louder, and our plans get a tad more outrageous. We may find ourselves plotting, and perhaps even carrying out, some daring plan. Like the women in the movie *9 to 5* who kidnapped their boss and transformed their workplace in his absence, put some like-minded women together, and there is no telling what will happen!

One woman shared this plan of revenge and wicked fun that she executed with her best friend: "I had been dating this man who had really treated me badly, and my girlfriend and I were furious about it. He drove a convertible which he cherished, so every night for a week we did something to that car. For example, one night we put smelly cheese on his front seat. Another night we attached a very large 'sexual aid' as a hood ornament so that the car resembled a unicorn. A different night, we left a bunch of narcissus on his windshield to make a statement about how self-centered he was, although I suspect the subtlety of that prank was beyond him. It was nevertheless satisfying to us. We had no intention of harming him or his car in any way, we just wanted to act out some frustration and laugh over a painful situation. It worked. Instead of feeling bad when I think of him now, I always get a grin on my face."

In the name of fun, girlfriends do a lot of healing. We laugh, we make plans, we take revenge, and as a result, we help each other recover from everything from bad moods to bad relationships. Tracey wrote us about how she helped Olivia heal from a romance that had undermined her self confidence: "Olivia and I met when I took a college job in a small jewelry store in Atlanta. We didn't become especially close until years later when she left an abusive relationship. Even though she had other friends, for some unknown reason, she turned to me to help her heal.

"Her healing process almost killed us both. She left this guy just before Christmas, so we celebrated both Christ's birth and her rebirth by going out on the town. She ended up with pneumonia and I got bronchitis! Now we think it is hilarious that we got sick from celebrating life!

"Perhaps one of the most healing things we did was to see several movies together. That following summer *Thelma and Louise* came out. That movie, along with *Fried Green Tomatoes* and *Steel Magnolias*, helped her to realize she was a powerful, creative force in this world and not a victim. I am still humbled that she chose to take me with her on that journey. By the way, has anyone ever noticed that the women in those three movies were all Southern? Being from the South, that fact was very significant in our lives. It was years before *Boys on the Side* came out depicting a Northern version, and even then, they went South."

Breakups with men seemed to be a theme in many of the outrageous stories we read. One woman suffered two traumatic events in her life at about the same time—a recent ending of an engagement and being held up at gun point at her own front door — and asked her friends to help her regain her sense of safety and power. Little did she know that these sobering events would leave them all with a lot of laughs and a memorable story.

She told us, "Looking back, the breakup was actually more traumatic than the holdup, although staring down the barrel of a gun was no thrill. The guy who held me up had the whole outfit, just like on TV, with the hooded sweat shirt and the ski mask. It was a warm time of year and the first thought that came to my mind when I saw him was, 'When you went to the ski equipment store to buy that ski mask, did they really think you were going skiing?' Fortunately I kept my mouth shut.

"After he left with my purse, the cops came and went, and everything had settled down, I thought I felt no fear. When friends would call and ask, 'Are you okay?' I'd say, 'Sure, I'm fine.' Then they'd say, 'You want to get together? Let's go out,' and I'd reply, 'I'm not leaving this house for the rest of my life.' As long as I stayed home, I could manage how scared I was, but the thought of being outside, vulnerable again, was unthinkable.

"After a couple of weeks of this, and my friends becoming tired of bringing me food, three girlfriends came over to help me get over this! Since I was still upset about my broken engagement, we decided to do a series of rituals for both events, with the hope of empowering me again. The first step was burning everything my ex had left behind. We went out behind my condo, threw his belongings into a large metal pot, and burned them while saying despicable things about him. This guy was a real health food nut and ate so many carrots that his skin was orange. After he left me, I couldn't stand the sight of carrots. So we got a bag of carrots, chewed them up and spit them into the burning pot. I really loved that part.

"Next we paraded around my front door where I'd been held up and declared this to be my safe space once again. I'm sure my neighbors thought I'd lost it. Here were four grown women marching around the complex like lunatics. Nevertheless, I felt much better and suggested we end our experience by sharing a cup of tea. In my mind, I envisioned powerful women over the ages sitting together in circles sipping tea and reminding each other of their strength. One of my girlfriends modified this picture by suggesting we share Diet Coke® instead, and everyone nodded in agreement.

"After the Diet Coke® was ceremoniously shared, and my girlfriends left, I felt totally different. These antics, that must appear ridiculous from the outside, helped me tremendously. While I'm still very cautious when I'm out alone, from that day forward I was never afraid to go about my business again. I reclaimed my personal power. Plus I felt so much better about letting go of my hurt over the breakup. Perhaps the best part is every time I eat carrots, I think about my girlfriends and smile rather than think of him and feel sad. That's a real gift."

For My Friend, I'll Try It!

As these stories indicate, we find ourselves doing things with a close girlfriend we probably would not do alone. The willingness to make a complete fool of yourself on either her or your behalf can be quite freeing. Holly told us this story of when she and her girlfriend Susan cooked up an overly complicated scheme to find out if a particular boy was at home. "There was this guy named Charlie that Susan liked in our freshman year of college. She had this major crush on him. We were home for vacation once, and she wanted to know if he had come home as well, but didn't want to be the one who called to find out. So she had me call him from my parents' phone, and she said, 'If he answers, just hang up, and if someone else answers, they will say "I'll go get him" at which point you can then hang up.' Then we revised it and decided that if he answered, I could pretend that we had call waiting and say, 'I've got another call.' We didn't actually have the call waiting service, so I was just going to hang up.

"I called the number and asked if he was there. 'Sure,' the guy says, 'This is Charlie.' I said, 'Uh, hold on a minute, I have another message,' which didn't make any sense whatsoever, so I just hung up. We were on the floor laughing, saying, 'Well, he's home! We know that!' I felt like a total idiot!" Although Holly felt "like an idiot," she and Susan nevertheless had fun. When we make a fool of ourselves with, and for, our friends, we get a good laugh and a sense of doing it for a good cause.

Lest we think that we need to be together to act crazy, consider Anette's story, sent to us from Germany. Anette, who missed her best friend in the United States, decided to involve both of them in a local radio contest, just to have some fun with her faraway friend. She wrote, "I was working in an office where we were allowed to listen to the radio. Every Thursday between 1 and 2 P.M. there's a show on the radio which is called 'Worldwidefaxing.' People from all over the world can send a fax to this German radio station, and the person sending the fax from the farthest distance during this hour wins a prize. When I heard this I immediately thought of Paula, my very best friend who lives in the United States. I was very excited to tell her about this contest.

"I will try almost anything, and because I know Paula is as crazy and spontaneous as me, I was quite sure she would send them a fax. She loved the idea of being on the German radio station, and she sent off her first fax. Our first try didn't go so well, due to a miscalculation of the time difference! Not to be discouraged, we decided to try again the next Thursday. But when Thursday arrived, Paula was so busy she had no time to send her fax.

"As they say, 'the third time is the charm,' and this was true for us. One Thursday when I wasn't expecting it, the telephone in our office rang, and a man from the radio station wanted to speak with me. I was shocked! He told me that he received a fax from my friend Paula and that he would call her soon so she could be live on air. To my surprise, he also wanted me on the air as well! This had never happened before on the show.

"At first I was a bit flustered, since I hadn't expected anything like that (it's one thing to push your girlfriend onto a radio show. It's altogether different when *you* have to talk too!) I really didn't want to talk over the radio with my best friend, especially since we would be speaking in English, not German. I was so terribly nervous and sure I would be at a loss for words or start crying or something. But I took a deep breath and told him I would do it.

"The man from the radio said he would call me back in a few minutes. I couldn't work after the phone call and waited and waited. Part of me would have been totally relieved if he had not called me again, because then I wouldn't have had to speak English over the air. But sure enough, he called me back and I was live on the radio. Then Paula started talking, and it was so wonderful to hear her voice. It was a very special moment, and all my colleagues shared it with me, because they listened too.

"It was funny to speak with Paula and the radio host on air and also terribly exciting. I was so proud of my fun experience! My mother taped our interview and now, whenever I miss Paula and want to listen to her voice, I can play the tape. Even though we're thousands of miles away from each other, we can still do crazy things together! Isn't that super? It's the greatest friendship I've ever had and I hope it will last always and forever!"

Regardless of culture or time or distance, we all bond together through laughter, dares, and crazy plans. Laughter is the evidence of the fun we are having in the moment, but can also be a sign of healing and keeping our balance as life throws us curve balls. A hearty belly laugh, one that brings tears to our eyes and leaves us gasping, can make a lot of evils disappear. Whether enjoying the wit and silliness of our friends, shedding our good-girl personas (or watching others become bad girls on the big screen), or sharing a live radio show, laughter and good times cleanses away a lot of trouble and heartache and just generally sweetens our existence. We can always find these tools of enjoyment—laughter, making trouble, and other healing measures—with our friends.

You Have Taught Me So Much

The bond that we forged so many years ago is now unbreak-able. And yes, she is still the person I most want to be like.

—GAYLE GOLDGLANTZ

Most lessons we learn from our girlfriends are rarely intended as "learning experiences." Rather, we teach by example, discover through observation, and glean new information from our continuing interactions. It is next to impossible to measure how much we end up learning from each other throughout our lifetimes. When we are young, our girlfriends may be the source of information about a great many subjects—sex, dating, grooming (not necessarily in that order). At any age, whether we discuss male-female relationships or hard drives, or watch as one friend deftly handles an awkward work situation, we gather knowledge from each other. Without necessarily intending to do so, we continually help each other get through yet another change-filled day.

Learning as We Go

Often our friends initially attract us with certain attributes we respect and enjoy. As we start spending more time together, we may then consciously try to adopt those characteristics we so admire. One woman, Kathy, wrote us and described how she has benefited from the examples of her girlfriends. She wrote, "For as long as I can remember, I've tried to imitate the best attributes of my friends and make them part of my own personality. My best high school friend laughed a lot and was always a happy person; consequently, from watching her, I try to be upbeat and make the best of situations. I realized that others enjoy being around happy people. My best friend and coworker during my first days of teaching school was a stylish woman who wore hats well. To this day I wear wide-brimmed hats and am often complimented. Another best friend from twenty years ago sold cosmetics at Saks Fifth Avenue. From her I learned the importance of wearing makeup, staying well groomed, and the secret of shopping the sales at only the best stores, two times a year, January and July, because of their incredible markdowns."

As Kathy points out, we can learn how to put on a smile, dress differently, and shop more effectively, from watching our girlfriends. But taking on new skills is just the tip of the iceberg. Girlfriends actually teach us much, much more.

Learning Our Value

Beneath the surface of learning "how to" accomplish a task, there is a deepening of a woman's self-esteem. One woman, Angela, talked about how her friend helped her feel more feminine: "I call my friend, Elizabeth, my manager. She has been teaching me how to make myself more of a priority, to better take care of myself. The examples of womanhood with which I was raised taught me that work always came first and that spending time on myself was frivolous. My aunts, grandmother, and mother all were very hard workers and not diligent about taking care of themselves. They neglected important tasks like getting regular medical checkups and making time for exercise, and the not-so-important things, like making sure their clothes made them feel attractive or that their cleansing cream was right for their skin type. Elizabeth knew that I was devoting all my time to work and feeling drained and unattractive, and for the last couple of years, she has made it a priority to go shopping with me. She was a design major in college and sold clothes for a long time in one of the more fashionable shops in town, so her eye is very discriminating.

"When I try on clothes now, if she thinks something looks attractive, she will say, 'I am not letting you leave without that blouse' or pants or whatever. We now joke about how bossy she is, my own personal shopper. She makes sure that I am using the right-colored lipstick. Whenever I buy something that she has recommended, I get great compliments. She also takes time to check things out for me, so I might get a call from her telling me I need to go to a particular store and try on a certain dress.

"One time she dragged me into a department store and would not let me leave until I got some new underwear before I went on a trip with my husband. I am touched that she takes the time from her own busy schedule to think about me. Plus I feel so much better about how I look now. By being encouraged to take time to pay attention to my appearance, I find I am also paying attention to how I feel. I have started exercising more, and just went to see my opthamologist and got new glasses for myself, something I have been putting off for two years."

The lessons we learn from our girlfriends are so powerful because they're taught through small, multiple acts of love. Elizabeth's attention to Angela's dissatisfaction with her appearance not only addressed that dissatisfaction, but also sent the message to Angela that she is worth Elizabeth's time and effort. When our friends show us this thoughtfulness, we more clearly recognize our own value as women and as human beings. Our sense of self grows more positive as we see ourselves through the eyes of our girlfriends; eyes filled with love. The message is that if they can like us, we can like ourselves!

Shaping Who We Are

Our friends not only teach us a sense of our value, but they often yield a powerful influence on our own development. Debbie told us how she believed her friend, Susan, was instrumental in shaping her personality at a young age. She said, "Susan wielded a lot of influence in my life and helped me gain confidence in myself, helping me to become more outgoing and gregarious and to hone my sense of humor. In retrospect, I think she was destined to be in my life at a time when I was having difficulties at home and needed such a friend."

We received quite a few letters expressing this sentiment, woman after woman sharing how she was shaped by her bond with other women. Sandra paid tribute to her dearest of friends when she wrote to us, "Eileen and I have shared so much together—we've been poor together, been devastated by our divorces together, and survived and healed together. Her old car, 'Luke the Buick' proved to be as unreliable as my old 1966 VW Beetle that sometimes got us where we were going, sometimes not. Most of the time, we didn't have much money to go anywhere anyway, so we just spent time together at each other's kitchen tables, sharing a cheap bottle of wine.

"We shared what little money we had, our clothes, our fears, our hopes, our dreams. As do many women going through divorce, we both lost a lot of weight. Eileen is the one who decided I needed a new hairdo to go with my new body. Not only did she highlight my hair and give me a great haircut, she continued to do my hair for the next fifteen years. She gave me so much more than a new hairstyle; she gave me a new image of myself and the base of a loving friendship. She helped me gain back my self-confidence. I can only hope that what I gave her in return helped, in some small part, to repay her for all of her kindness and love."

Sandra's story illustrates how something as simple as a new hairstyle can begin to transform a woman's view of herself, especially if it is given by a loving friend. Our friends affect our personalities, our appearances, and how we feel about ourselves in general. We look to our girlfriends to help us make sense of ourselves as women, which in this society often translates into how we look. Women talk to each other about their bodies—how they're shaped, how they're aging, how we feel about them—in an effort to cope with the unrealistic and demanding expectations of perfection we are confronted with every day. We discuss our weight, dieting, exercise, clothes sizes, and our feelings about being too much or too little. We can be honest with our girlfriends because we know that no matter how we look, we're accepted warts and all. With our girlfriends cheering us on, bolstering our courage and, when we make mistakes, assuaging our guilt, we may learn that we do not have so many "warts" after all!

Learning the Truth About Ourselves

Often we do not have a true picture of ourselves, and it is the women we let close to us who help us see ourselves more clearly. Vicky, a poet and leader of women's groups, told us about the transformation she saw in Kelly due to the support she was given in one of Vicky's classes. She said, "I teach a class, for women only, called 'In the Mirror, Women Facing the Possibility of Their Beauty' in which we combine poetry writing and nude photography. Each woman designs her own photo shoot that may include sacred or symbolic objects. There is no emphasis on fashion, or trying to look like a centerfold. Rather, we are exploring our intrinsic beauty as women. It's amazing how over the years my mind has been trained to see traditional beauty. On whose authority is this line more beautiful than this curve? Who said this face is more attractive than that? And when did I swallow a particular standard? I help my students question their assumptions about beauty.

"One of my students, Kelly, is very large, over two-hundred fifty pounds, and absolutely, stunningly beautiful. Because of her weight, Kelly Anna could not even think of herself as beautiful in any way. With the support of the group, and the particular help of one woman, La Nette, who teamed up with her for their photo shoots, Kelly brought items that meant a great deal to her, her grandmother's hand-crocheted bedspread and a white porcelain bowl. The experience of the photo shoot was very healing for her.

"When her photos came back, all the women in the class gasped at the beauty of them. Kelly couldn't see it. She said, 'The photo shoot was so dramatic, I somehow thought that when the photos came back, I'd be a size ten.' When she wasn't, she could only see herself as large and unattractive.

"At the same time she was opening herself up to the possibility of being beautiful, she started dating a man who saw her as the magnificent woman she was. She told him about the difficulties she was having in the class. He echoed what the women in the class had told her—that she was stunning. Right before the end of that series of classes, she came in and told me he'd asked her to marry him. She said that because of the support of the women in the class, her self esteem had risen so much that she could finally imagine someone loving her. They married soon after and I got to go to the wedding. She and her husband now use the porcelain bowl to wash each other's hands for Passover. And we use her photograph on our brochure. It's one of the most beautiful photographs I've ever seen anywhere."

Seeing Ourselves in a New Light

Our friends can help us view ourselves more positively because they are an honest mirror to see ourselves more accurately. The women who love us with a lifelong commitment often have the boldness to tell it like it is. Jane told us, "I've always seen myself as someone who is open-minded, and not particularly opinionated, when I discuss things with other people. However, I've frequently taken the role of devil's advocate, saying something like, 'Well, what if something else happens?' or 'Have you thought about it from this angle?' So I was really surprised when a friend of mine said to me, 'I nearly always go along with what you say because you always sound like you know what you're talking about. You have such firm opinions.'" It can be a revelation to discover how others perceive us, a revelation that makes us sit back and reconsider our actions.

One woman told us how her friend helped her see herself in a new light: "I always had the feeling that I was the person who was not taken seriously, that I was ineffectual. If I was angry I didn't feel that I was heard. My friend Lily and I work together, and I found myself confessing this frustrating feeling to her over drinks after work one night. She just looked at me incredulously and said, 'Do you really think that?' and added, 'Well, I don't ever want you angry with me!' I laughed because I thought of Lily as the tough one, someone who had a more powerful personality than me. But her comments got us talking and she told me that her perception was that I had a great deal of respect from my coworkers, and was not perceived as weak. She convinced me by saying, 'Come on, do you think I would be best friends with the person you are describing?' That was convincing, and my perception of myself in my professional capacity started shifting. Her view of me was quite different than how I thought I came across to others."

Seeing ourselves differently, from the vantage

points of our friends, can be so powerful at times, it can literally alter our perspectives on life. Perhaps most profound is the realization that we are not alone. Carmen, one of the authors of this book, recently experienced such a transformation: "I once read a quote in *The Harper Book of Quotations* from Agnes Macphail that said, 'We meet all life's greatest tests alone.' On an existential level, I suspect we all feel alone, as there are experiences that no one can have for us. In some ways, I believe I've felt this solitariness more strongly because I am an only child. In my family, the responsibility of caring for my parents ultimately falls on my shoulders — mine alone.

"The weight of this responsibility became nearly unbearable last year when my father had a serious accident and, four months later, died. I went into that experience feeling very much the only child but have emerged knowing that I have many, many sisters. For example, Alice, whom I met in the fourth grade but had lost contact with, came back into my life a short time before my dad's accident. Now a surgeon, Alice was invaluable in talking with my father's physicians and helping me ask the right questions. Right after the accident, Tamara, my detail-oriented cowriter, jumped on a plane and spent several days with me at the hospital, getting the practical side of my life in order. Cathy, whom I met in 1978, called me daily with the newest information she had discovered to help me make decisions about my dad's care, giving me an emotional home base to voice my worst fears. Another friend I met in 1978, Irene, was battling cancer through chemotherapy and radiation, yet she made sure I took my vitamins and kept my sense of humor. Pat, who has been in my life for fourteen years, showed up at the hospital regularly to check in on my mother and me, without ever needing to be asked. One of my newer friends, Marianne, spent entire nights at the hospital caring for my father when I was too tired to take another step. The weekend my father died, Gail, a friend for over twenty years, came in from out of town and held me while I cried. Flying and driving in from all over the country, my girlfriends participated in the memorial service — Rene, whom I met in college, played his favorite hymns on the organ; Cynthia, who's been my buddy since we were both ten years old, sang like an angel; and Lynn, a close friend for the last five years, led us all in the Lord's Prayer.

"I may be the only child of David and Ellen Berry, but I am not alone. I am surrounded by women who love me as a sister and give to me without measuring the effort. They have taught me what Agnes apparently never learned — when we have lifelong girlfriends, we never go through life's tests by ourselves. Our friends are always by our side."

You Nudge Me
in the Right Direction

*At the age of forty-nine, I decided to follow a dream of perform-
ing music, a dream I'd had all my life. I couldn't have made it
without the encouragement of my friends. An unexpected gift
was that my girlfriends saw my success and that inspired
several of them to go after their potential. It's a thrill to see
them so happy and fulfilled.*

—LINDA MCKECHNIE

Because keeping friends for the rest of your life requires learning to overcome changes and challenges,
these important relationships often become the cata-
lysts for our personal growth. Our connection with
our girlfriends introduces us to new experiences, ideas,
and attitudes and can be the impetus to embark on
exciting adventures, whether it is traveling halfway
around the world or taking a fresh path in our emotional or career lives.

Unspoken Influence

Many of us recall the "culture shock" of going to our girlfriends' homes for the first time as children. New rules, new people, and new routines open our eyes to the truth that different individuals and families organize their lives differently. Being included in a friend's life and family may be our first mind-opening experience as we are introduced to lifestyles, manners, and surroundings we have never before seen.

Carolyn talked about how just spending the night at her friend's house when she was a little girl was an adventure for her: "Kristi lived in a home that had both parents and a younger brother. It was always different to spend the night at their house, because in my house I didn't have a father who lived at home. My parents got divorced when I was five, and my mother never remarried. I was so nervous the first time I spent the night at Kristi's house. We were eating spaghetti, and I was shaking so much I flipped my noodle into my milk glass and my fork ended up on the floor. We still to this day laugh about it." Carolyn was introduced to the presence of a full-time father in the house by visiting her friend Kristi. While this new experience made the little girl nervous, she benefited from watching how Kristi related to her father, and the knowledge that "family" means something different to each person.

Pushing Our Boundaries

As adults, we can find that a girlfriend's presence encourages us to experience things we might not otherwise. As Karen told us, "Martina is my very special, international girlfriend. I am an American from Boston, Martina is Irish and from Dublin. We met in Ghana, West Africa, where our husbands were working together building the first thermal power plant in the country. Martina and I hit it off from the first day we met. It was a perfect match of two women who found themselves isolated under unique and limited surroundings. We were both twenty-nine years of age, recently married, and had no children. We both left our careers in hotels and nursing to move to Ghana and live with our husbands. We clicked and formed a special bond that has turned into a friendship of a lifetime.

"Over a period of eight months, we explored a foreign and very unfamiliar country by foot and car. We met people from countries worldwide and made acquaintances with people who taught us their culture. We took various lessons including golf, tennis, and French. We shopped everywhere for everything. Amongst all that, we spent time just hanging out and talking, whether it was at the beach, in the car, over coffee or drinks at a restaurant, or at our homes.

"This journey into the unknown together created a truly deep friendship that will continue from our homelands. We will always be 'sisters,' as the locals referred to us; we were always together. When one of us was without the other, a local in town would always ask where the other sister was. Together we learned much and helped each other through a very wonderful and extraordinary experience abroad."

We were surprised at how many letters we received describing vibrant, even life-changing friendship between women from different countries and cultures. Often beginning in girlhood through a pen-pal program, these international duos continued their writings well into adulthood, sharing various experiences in spite of language difficulties or possible misinterpretation due to cultural differences.

Anette sent us this story about how she and her best friend Paula met and challenged each other to build a friendship that crossed miles and cultures. She wrote, "It all started over fourteen years ago. I was eleven, living in southern Germany, and enrolled in my first English class at school, where we had a chance to get a pen pal from another country. All I had to do was to write down my name, address, age, hobbies, and the country where I wanted a pen pal. I wanted a pen friend who wrote German, a girl around my age. We sent off all the information to an organization in

Finland, and then we waited to see what would happen. I got a pen pal from Austria, but also got a surprise—a pen pal named Paula from the United States!

"A few weeks later I received a letter from Paula. I remember the day exactly: the twenty-fourth of December, 1984. My first thought when I looked at the letter and the picture was: 'What terrible handwriting, and what a pretty, sweet blond girl! When I think back on it now, I realize that this letter from Paula was the greatest Christmas present I had ever gotten in my life!

"We wrote each other about once a month, although sometimes it took Paula two or three months to write me back, because she was so busy (I think mostly with boys). We wrote about things like school, friends, holidays, hobbies, the weather, and our plans for the next weeks. We sent each other little gifts and nice cards for birthdays and Christmas. We exchanged pictures, stickers, newspapers, and other things—it was always so exciting to receive things from so far away.

"After writing regularly to each other for over five years, Paula's letters stopped coming. I couldn't believe that she stopped writing to me. I wrote her again, but nothing happened. I gave up but never forgot her.

"One day in November, after I didn't hear from

her for over a year and a half, I received a letter from Paula, and I couldn't believe my eyes. She apologized profusely, explaining that she had found her dream man, had fallen totally in love, and had forgotten everything else. I was so happy to hear from her again and readily forgave her. Our friendship became even stronger. We wrote letters regularly, and when we both got access to fax machines, hundreds of faxes were exchanged. I cannot thank the inventor of the fax machine enough!

"Finally, my biggest wish came true—to meet Paula. Together with my friend Sybille, we planned a visit to see Paula in Michigan and Sybille's friend in Pennsylvania. From the moment I was sure that I'd see Paula, we wrote about it in every letter. We planned our time together, what we wanted to do and visit. Paula sent me brochures and prepared a wonderful adventure in the States.

"As the big day came closer, I was both happy and nervous—nervous because I wondered if being with her would be different than I imagined, and happy because, even though we'd never met, she was my dearest friend. After all the planning, I couldn't believe that I was actually standing in the Chicago airport, seeing her for the first time.

"At first we were both at a loss for words because I was not used to speaking English. Writing in English is no problem for me, since I can take my time, but talking is much harder. But it didn't take long before we were talking about the flight and our plans. From hour to hour and from day to day we had more to talk about. We had so much fun together. All was perfect and my anxieties and hesitations were for nothing. I got to know her parents, sister, husband, and in-laws—all the people I only knew from Paula's letters. All was so natural, and it seemed that we had been together always.

"Both of us cried terribly when I left. It's always hard to say goodbye to a person you love, but it's especially hard to say goodbye when you don't know when you will see her again. Maybe in Germany? I don't know."

Through their letters, Anette and Paula experienced each other's cultures, and Anette was inspired to visit the United States. Anette may never have traveled halfway around the world had not her beloved Paula been there to welcome her. Knowing that our girlfriends will be there for us during the journey can be the inspiration we need to take risks we have only imagined.

The opportunity of meeting a pen pal, or seeing the physical surroundings of someone they know so well but have never actually met, has motivated quite a few women to travel the world. Wendy told us this story: "Everyone thought I was out of my mind when they heard, in January 1996, that I was planning to travel by myself to the other side of the planet to stay with someone I'd never met. But it was something I'd dreamt about for six years — ever since my Australian pen pal Michelle and I started exchanging letters.

"As a kid, Australia enchanted me. It seemed like such an unusual place, home to all sorts of strange wildlife and creatures. I always wanted to learn more about it by corresponding with an Australian pen pal, and in my twenties I finally went about getting one. I remember the first letter Michelle sent me. She sounded fun and animated, writing, 'I'd be happy to answer your questions about Australia and set those rumors straight!' Well, that began a friendship that evolved slowly from polite inquiries about each other's life to lengthy discussions about religion, relationships, and family problems. Although we were thousands of miles away, we discovered that we were amazingly (and sometimes almost frighteningly) alike.

"Soon it seemed we were writing epics to each other, and we found verbal messages on cassette tapes to be a much more efficient way to share our news. We also exchanged videotapes and e-mail and spoke on the phone a few times.

"Then came my trip Down Under. When I met Michelle in the airport, we were laughing, talking, and

```
SUPER CROWN #735

01/20/01  14:22        G          12       12804
         EVERYTHING DISCOUNTED, EVERY DAY
         PUBLISHER             CROWN     CROWN
         PRICE                SAVINGS    PRICE
GIRLFRIENDS FOR LIFE
 1@ 13.95  1885171323        10%        12.56
SUBTOTAL                          $     12.56
SALES TAX @ 6.75%                 $      0.85
TOTAL                             $     13.41
TENDERED Check                    $     13.41

        YOUR SAVINGS AT CROWN... $ 1.39
```

walking through the airport with our arms around each other's shoulders when she turned to me and said, 'Isn't this strange. We've really only just met!' It truly was strange to meet someone who was simultaneously my best friend and a stranger. I had the most amazing time on my trip, petting kangaroos, seeing the constellations of the southern hemisphere in the night sky, and other new experiences. But the best part of my trip, of course, was just being with my friend, talking, shopping, and sharing her Australian world.

"This summer, 'Shell' came to see me in New York. I took her to see the sights. One of her favorite things was experiencing firsthand the sales, fireworks, and general hoopla of Independence Day. I guess one of the most poignant moments I had during her visit was when I introduced her to someone as my pen pal, and Michelle said offhandedly, 'Oh no, we're more than that now.'"

Unselfish Support

The desire to meet a friend and get to know her better can push us to adventures that we may not have embarked on without her. Just as the presence of a girlfriend a continent away can inspire us to travel and expand our world view, so our friends close to home can encourage us to embrace all that life has to offer, even if it takes us away from them.

One of the true tests of friendship is asking for support and encouragement from a girlfriend in making a decision that results in leaving that girlfriend behind. Heidi, an Austrian woman, sent us a moving letter, telling us about how her two closest girlfriends have supported her in following a lifelong dream of moving from Austria to the United States. Heidi told us that while she was born in Vienna, she lived the first years of her life in New Jersey, until her parents divorced. She and her mother, who is originally from Austria, returned to Vienna, and Heidi would visit her father in the United States in the summer and during winter holidays.

Heidi went on to describe her dearest friends in Vienna, Karin and Tina: "We've known each other for twenty years, since we were ten years old. I was the new kid in class, and they immediately befriended me. We went through many fights and tears in school, lost touch for a couple of years as we all went on to different schools, and then found each other again in our late teens.

"A few years back, I had my heart broken for the first time. Karin and Tina were there. I phoned Tina, and I doubt she understood anything as I sobbed into the phone, but she got in her car and came right over.

It was at a late hour, and she stayed the night because I couldn't bear to be alone. She left sometime during the day, when Karin came over to stay the next night. I felt like I didn't want to live anymore, and they showed me how silly that was. I ask myself if they have ever needed me the way I needed them during that time. I hope they know I am there for them the way they were for me. I think that's what it's about — knowing that you are there for each other and accepting their help and not having to wonder how or when you can pay them back.

"Now, years later, they are both married, and Karin has two little girls. Tina also has a baby girl. When I go out with either of the two couples, I never feel like a third wheel. I get along great with their husbands. We do a lot together — social activities, skiing, daytrips to the country, movies, and the museum. I feel like part of the family.

"Even though we have been so close for so long, I told them about eighteen months ago that I wanted to move to New York to try out living in a different country. It was very hard for me to think about leaving Karin and Tina. But because they are such true friends, they did not try to hold me back. Even though we all would miss our times together, they both encouraged me to do what I've wanted to do for a long time. The distance can never do any harm to our friendship. It helps me a lot to know we will always be best friends."

Karin and Tina pass the test of true friendship, to be certain. Only those who really love you can encourage you to follow your dream or take a step that is good for you, even if it means they will not be with you as much as they perhaps would like. This kind of support can further strengthen an already strong bond and is a good sign that a friendship will last.

Giving Us Confidence

The most challenging and certainly most frightening adventure we can embark upon is one that brings risk into our lives. This kind of adventure involves taking a path that requires us to live our lives in a different way. Many people dream of making changes or going after goals that seem beyond their grasp, but few have the courage, confidence, or self-esteem to single-handedly make these dreams a flesh-and-blood reality. Girlfriends can give us the extra push we need to go to those strange territories, to say 'no' when we want to, to say 'yes' when we want to (both without guilt), to set our boundaries, and to just generally live in a way more beneficial to ourselves.

Lydia wrote us about how frightened she was the night before an important job interview, and how

Sidra, her dear friend, helped her ace that interview. Lydia said, "I was a complete mess. I'd just graduated from art school, and I always had a fantasy of working in animated features. Even as a little girl, going to the movies and watching those huge images on the screen, I dreamed of creating worlds of myth and legend. And here I was, the night before the big interview with the company I most wanted to work for, and all I could do was shake and tell myself I was a fool for going for it.

"Fortunately, Sidra called, and when I answered she could hear by the quavering in my voice that I was a basket case. 'I'm coming right over,' she said and hung up before I could protest. To be honest, I didn't want her over when I felt so insecure. But she came anyway, bringing a pizza so I wouldn't go hungry (she knows that when I get nervous I lose my appetite). On top of the pizza box was a large cardboard portfolio.

"Once we started eating, she opened the portfolio and brought out drawings and paintings I had done over the years and had given to her. She held one up and described how the image moved her, pointed to another and told me what it meant to her, and so on until she had gone through the entire stack. I just sat there in stunned silence. When she was finished, she said, 'Lydia, you are an incredible artist. Don't ever doubt that. You have everything it takes to realize your dream.'

"I took a deep breath and realized I was no longer anxious. She had tricked me out of my fear. The sense of confidence she gave me that night lasted well into the next day. In fact, I was so calm during the interview I surprised myself. I got the job, and I know that I owe it, in part, to Sidra and the way she encouraged me the night before the interview. I knew in my heart she meant every word. She really did think I was capable, and her confidence energized me to believe I was, too."

Rose told us about how her friend took the time to encourage her about her abilities to be a good mother: "When I first got pregnant, my girlfriend kept saying so sincerely what a wonderful mom she thought I would be. She started saying things like, 'You know, if you are half as good at nurturing your child as you are at nurturing your friends, you are going to be the best mother.' She listed all these qualities that she thought I have that would make me a good mom. I got choked up. I was so stunned."

By naming specific qualities that Rose possessed, Rose knew that her friend was not making rote statements of support. Her specificity and attention to Rose's attributes got Rose's attention and helped boost her confidence in her mothering ability. Just paying attention to our friends and letting them know that they are ready to take the next step in their lives (then being able to list the reasons why) can help them to go in the right direction.

Keeping Us on the Right Path

Some goals are set under difficult circumstances, in situations we had not anticipated. Lynn told us how her life had fallen apart after "going through a messy breakup and being very disappointed with men, myself, and God. But you never know where help will come from when God is taking care of you. Sometimes it can be from an obvious source, like a church, or just a hug from your niece. I have most recently felt God's loving touch through my girlfriend Heather who is a beautiful person inside and out. She's physically gorgeous on the outside, but it hasn't always been that way. At one time in her life she was on the really heavy side. She has worked very hard to slim down to have a very fit body. I think part of the reason she is so beautiful on the inside is because of her struggles.

"Like Heather, I have also struggled with this food battle for all my adult life. When my relationship broke up, my disappointment turned into a desire for food. I rekindled some old bad friendships with doughnuts, tacos, and ice cream. The closer these friendships got, the worse I felt and the sadder I became. I wanted to exercise and start eating right, but I just didn't have the energy to do anything. I'm one of those people who truly hates to exercise, and being an extrovert, I had to have somebody to exercise with me. I used the fact that I didn't have anyone to work out with as an excuse. When Heather heard that—to my chagrin— she jumped right in and volunteered!

"Not paying attention to my excuses, Heather talked me into meeting her at her gym and, as a Christmas present, bought me a month's membership with the condition that I go six days a week. She was so sweet that I felt I had to agree, thinking to myself, 'Why are you agreeing to exercise, you idiot? You hate this!' Heather is such a giver, and I am a person who tries to keep my word, so before I knew it . . . I was committed.

"We are now at the end of the month, and except for the four days I was sick, I have kept my word. It has been a lifesaver. I have made new friends at the gym; I see my body changing, even though my eating habits are still a struggle; and I can see my world getting better as my body gets thinner. I am especially grateful to God for providing not only a girlfriend, but a girlfriend who has kept her word and her enthusiasm when it would have been so much easier to do her own thing and let me wallow in depression. She has definitely nudged me in the right direction. God bless you, Heather, The Exercise Queen!"

When our friends see us making self-destructive choices, they can encourage us to re-evaluate how we are treating ourselves. And when tragedy strikes, our friends can help us overcome our losses with positive change. Kathie told us about how her friend not only helped her survive the loss of two babies, but later encouraged her to pursue a career in which she was interested. She said, "Soon after I met Lisa in 1979, when she became engaged to my brother, I went to the hospital to deliver my daughter Sarah. I'm sad to say that Sarah died before I delivered her. Lisa, who was a nurse at that same hospital, came to visit me with my brother. She stayed with me and made sure I had the best care possible.

"When I went home, Lisa called and checked in on me daily. I came to depend on her knowledge and support. Four months later, I became pregnant again. In December of 1980, I delivered a beautiful little girl named Katie. Lisa was with me in the delivery room and took care of Katie in the nursery. My friends and family were in the room with me, celebrating Katie's birth, when Lisa entered the room and told me Katie was having problems. Lisa called in one of the best heart specialists to see Katie and within two hours of her birth, my little girl went to have heart surgery—with Lisa by her side. Four hours after Katie was born, Lisa entered my hospital room to tell me my daughter had died during surgery.

"Through these terrible losses, Lisa has become my soul mate. She encouraged me through my grief. Due to her support, I gained enough confidence to go to nursing school myself. I was so impressed with how much Lisa had helped me. Without her example, I don't know how I would have made it through these experiences, and I doubt that I would ever have made it to nursing school.

"In turn, I have been able to be with Lisa through the loss of her son and the premature births of both her beautiful sons. We now work together daily at the hospital. She is my supervisor in the emergency room, where I work as a nurse. The day I met Lisa, a dark hole in my life was filled. She is my sister in the truest sense of the word. For nineteen years, our conversations have ended with, 'Don't worry. You'll be fine.' When I am with Lisa, I *am* fine."

Kathie's experiences could easily have pushed her into an abyss of grief, difficult to escape. Lisa provided the lifeline Kathie needed—being present, assuring her that she would survive, and focusing Kathie on a new goal. Our friends for life gently keep us on track, even when life's events seem too much to bear.

A Continuing Cycle

A little bit of nudging can go a long way. The encouragement we provide a friend often cycles back to inspire us as we see her accomplishing her goals. The following story illustrates how the support Linda received for pursuing her dreams helped her achieve them. In turn, her accomplishments have resulted in encouraging her friends to identify what they want and grow as individuals. Now in her fifties, Linda told us that when she was a young woman she had three dreams. The first two were to "be a wife and mother, which came true early in my life when I married my husband, who is a pastor, and then had my children. However, my third dream took about twenty years to happen. I am a pianist, and I've always wanted to record my music.

"I have been very involved in my husband's ministry and in raising my family. It wasn't until I was forty-nine that I signed my first music contract. I just turned fifty-seven and within the last eight years, I've enjoyed a great deal of success. I've just finished recording my sixth album. The congregation has witnessed this major change from me being a wife and mother and directing the choir of the church to suddenly being well known around the country and traveling a lot. It's been so wonderful to have my friends so excited about my success. I feel that true friends celebrate your successes without being jealous.

"An exciting side benefit of my success is how it's affected some of my girlfriends. Some of my friends had not finished college and, as they became empty nesters, they did not feel fulfilled in their own lives. They saw me being fulfilled by pursuing my dreams, so two of them decided to go back to college and get their degrees. They are both married to financially successful men, so neither of them felt pressured to go back to school, but they saw what I was doing with my life, traveling alone and feeling very confident in what I was doing, and they decided if I could do it, so could they!

"One friend in particular had wanted to travel but was nervous about traveling by herself, especially internationally. But she really wanted to study in England, so she went there by herself, and her husband came over and visited her a couple of times. She saw from the way that I was living that she could do the same thing, too.

"Another friend went on to get a masters in psychology and counseling, and she is now the executive director of a counseling center. Her life is so much happier and fulfilling. It is so much fun for me to see them just love what they are doing. So it feels like because of my success, they have decided they wanted to do the same thing. I was very surprised when each woman told me I was her inspiration. It's a humbling thing to know that they have encouraged me and that I, in turn, have encouraged them."

We learned that Linda's story is not exaggerated when we talked with Sally, one of her girlfriends, and found that Linda has, through her example and support, nudged several women in the direction right for them. Sally told us, "Last spring, my husband, Steve, and I talked about going to Hawaii for a vacation. Our last child was graduating from college, so our checkbook was going to have a plus sign instead of a minus for the first time in four years.

"One evening Steve came home after talking with our pastor, Linda's husband, and told me that we'd been invited to go on an African mission trip instead of Hawaii. I immediately answered 'Yes!' then asked myself, 'Where did that come from?' I had imagined being on a beach in Hawaii with my husband on a second honeymoon. Instead, I was going to Africa where sometimes there was no hot water, where I'd be traveling with twenty-one people I didn't know, and where I'd be helping Linda with her concerts and singing songs I'd never heard before. I was way out of my comfort zone.

"I'm so grateful that Linda asked me to help her with her musical concerts, even though music is not ne of my talents. I helped Linda give four concerts. One of them was in a Nairobi orphanage, where all of the children had birth defects and had been abandoned. There were two hundred children at the orphanage, and their voices sounded better than any choir.

"I sat right in the middle of them, and they just beamed. All they wanted was someone to sit there with them. One finally turned to me and said, 'Can we touch your hair?' So they started stroking me like they would a lion or a cat. They had never seen blond hair before. It was an amazing experience.

"Since I've been back, I have heard from some of them. They will write me and just say, 'We were blessed because you were here. Thank you.' Since those two wonderful weeks in Africa, I hum the tunes I learned there and listen to the tape of those children's voices. My wish is that when someone asks you to leave your comfort zone, you will do what I did and answer from your heart."

When someone believes in us, especially if that someone is a girlfriend who knows us at our worst and best, her faith can be the ground upon which our self-confidence is built. Her belief can provide the courage for us to take on new conquests and adventures. After all, who knows us better? If they believe in us, who are we to doubt them—one of the reasons that we chose each other as girlfriends is because of our excellent discernment and taste, not to mention sound judgment!

How many of us would be where we are today, with the accomplishments we have obtained, without our girlfriends telling us "I know you can do it!"? When we take that daring trip, put out our hand to receive that diploma, or walk into an office for an interview for that coveted job, we know that our girlfriends share in the sweet taste of victory. They have helped us get this far—what is next?

Women Speak

Women speak
through the invisible membranes
that keep us separate,
distant from each other.
Your voice
comes in like a salve
to an unseeable wound.
We are used to letting
someone into us
and so we let each other's
hope,
make room for
each other's vulnerability,
begin to see
its actual strength.
This ink
which shares us more
lets eyes see in
to the possibility in themselves.
We point to what
is broken and mended
and true,
when women speak.

—Vicky Edmonds

About the Authors

CARMEN RENEE BERRY is a nationally certified body-worker, former psychotherapist, and the author of ten books including *When Helping You Is Hurting Me, Coming Home to Your Body*, and *Is Your Body Trying to Tell You Something?*. Carmen has an M.S.W. from the University of Southern California and an M.A. in Social Sciences from Northern Arizona University. She resides in Sierra Madre, California.

TAMARA TRAEDER is a publisher, author, and intellectual property attorney. Tamara graduated from the University of Virginia Law School in 1985, and from the University of Missouri with a liberal arts degree in 1982. She lives in Berkeley, California.

Carmen and Tamara's other *girlfriends* books are *girlfriends: Invisible Bonds, Enduring Ties, The girlfriends Keepsake Book: The Story of Our Friendship*, and *girlfriends Talk About Men: Sharing Secrets for a Great Relationship*. They enjoy a rich and rewarding friendship from opposite ends of California.

Wildcat Canyon Press publishes books that embrace such subjects as friendship, spirituality, women's issues, and home and family, all with a focus on self-help and personal growth. Great care is taken to create books that inspire reflection and improve the quality of our lives. Our books invite sharing and are frequently given as gifts.

For a catalog of our publications, please write:

WILDCAT CANYON PRESS
2716 Ninth Street
Berkeley, California 94710
Phone: (510) 848-3600
Fax: (510) 848-1326
Circulus@aol.com